Enterprise Application
Integration Architecture
in corporate IT

beyond technology

Piet Knijnenburg

Osiris ITS
Overpelterbaan 61
3940 Hechtel-Eksel
Belgium

ISBN: 978-90-829099-1-3

Table of Contents

1   Preface 1

    1.1   Why bother? 7

    1.2   Audience 7

    1.3   Takeaways 8

2   Introduction 9

3   History 15

    3.1   Architecture in IT 18

4   The Problem Space 23

5   The Solution Space 29

    5.1   Systems of systems 32

    5.2   Complexity 34

    5.3   Loose coupling 36

    5.4   The systemic approach 41

    5.5   Business process modeling 49

    5.6   The Vitruvius principles 54

6   The integration stack 58

    6.1   Authentication & Authorization 60

    6.2   Transport Protocol 62

    6.3   Transport Security 63

    6.4   Data Structure or technical information content 67

    6.5   Message Exchange Pattern or MEP 70

    6.6   Policies 73

    6.7   Information Type or functional information content 77

    6.8   Business Process protocols and Workflow 82

    6.9   Service Level Requirement/Agreement 84

7   Synthesis 86

    7.1   Data Integration 88

    7.2   Application Integration 94

7.3   Versioning... 133

8   About tooling. 139

8.1   Service Composition, Service Orchestration & Process Choreography... 144

8.2   Integration as a platform.. 146

9   The Integration Architect... 152

9.1   The traditional integration architect 154

9.2   The guerilla integration architect............................. 155

10   Bibliography.. 158

1 Preface

This century the term "Architecture" has become a buzz-word in the information technology community. Especially the terms "Software architecture", "Enterprise architecture" and "Solution architecture" are ubiquitous. Enterprise architecture positions itself as the coordinating umbrella over the various architecture domains, and most of the enterprise architecture frameworks recognize the same domains: "Business architecture", "Data architecture", "Application architecture" and "Technology architecture". Integration architecture is rarely mentioned, and if it is at all mentioned, it is often considered to be a subdomain of Technology architecture. The question arises whether Integration architecture can be recognized as a valid architecture domain, or is just an aspect of another architecture domain. Before we can answer this question, we must know what the integration architecture domain comprises.

Almost every medium-sized to large organization will probably have a collection of enterprise systems and enterprise applications that need to communicate and cooperate to support the organizations primary and secondary business processes. As such it can be compared to a team of football-players. If every player has his or her own vision, strategy and tactics, then as a team you leave it to happenstance whether your players can communicate and cooperate enough to succeed. They probably won't. We understand that a perfectly attuned team of average players is more valuable than a collection of individual star players that do not know how to cooperate. Success of the team depends on a shared vision, strategy and tactics, and it is the task of a coach to develop and communicate the vision, strategy and tactics, and to ensure that the players implement it correctly. In exactly the same way, the smooth communication and cooperation between enterprise systems and applications is more important than the systems and applications themselves. Organizations need a "coach" to develop and communicate a vision, strategy and tactics to the owner(s) of the enterprise systems and applications. This "coach" is enterprise architecture, or more precise, the IT facing aspect of enterprise architecture, and the vision and strategy are derived from the vision, strategy and tactics from the business facing aspect of enterprise architecture. An organization where this role of enterprise architecture is not addressed, is like a collection of individual football-players without a coach. As simplistic as this analogy seems to be, it is a profound one. A network of well-integrated applications will support your business processes better than an unplanned collection of best-of-breed applications.

After the initial automation efforts in the past we are now making the shift from corporate IT registering business processes to corporate IT supporting business processes. The most progressive organizations are evolving towards the next step: the shift from corporate IT supporting business processes to corporate IT participating in business processes. This is the quintessential characteristic of what is now known under the hype-term 'digital transformation': evolution to the digital enterprise is not left to the IT department, but is regarded as an integral part of operational business management. 'Digital Transformation' is the assimilation of corporate IT into operational business management.

Other current hype-terms are 'microservices' and 'API's', which are positioned as the motor for 'Digital Transformation'. Apparently they are the solution to all integration issues. Without going into too much detail, microservices and API's are *techniques* to allow clients to use these services and API's, for example to request data from them, or to let them perform some action. The *techniques* however are not the problem. What we need to know is when and when not to use them, where and where not to use them, how and how not to use them, what information they should and should not be processing. There is a remarkable lack of guidance in these aspects, not just specifically for microservices and API's, but for integration solutions in general.

While we are making the shift from registering business processes to supporting business processes we must observe that the registration of business processes is inherently very much data driven; information associated with business processes is analyzed, data-models are conceived, and software is designed to record and retrieve data to and from these data-models. While this concept was successful for the first generations of software development, it no longer serves the demands of supporting business processes, let alone the demands of participating in business processes. In these latter cases, data modeling plays second violin to business process modeling.

Traditionally the IT department would suffice with observing business processes or eliciting business requirements, after which they could step back and design, build and deploy a solution in isolation. Contrarily, IT participation means that business processes are (re)engineered to capitalize on information technology in a joined effort in which IT and non-IT workers cooperate. Integration will ineluctably play a crucial role in this playground. An early, well-known example of this is JIT (just-in-time) logistics, where integration of supplier and customer IT solutions would allow a drastic reduction or even elimination of warehouses and logistical processes.

In old school IT, application integration meant transferring data from one datastore to another. With this simplistic approach you can defend that integration architecture is an aspect of technology and solution architecture, and does not merit recognition as an independent architecture domain. More and more organizations are aware of the significance of good communication and cooperation between enterprise applications. Through technological advancement connectivity between enterprise applications is nowadays better than ever before. But connectivity alone is not good enough, the most important aspect of communication is that the communication partners understand each other. For understanding each other they need to have a common language, a common vocabulary and a common interpretation of terminology.

In an applications network, just understanding each other is insufficient: it is nothing more than a prerequisite to cooperation. And just as understanding is a prerequisite, so is coordination. Even if you can understand each other perfectly, without some form of coordination you cannot achieve effective cooperation.

We must observe that almost all of-the-shelf ERP systems that call themselves well integrated, in reality are not. Indeed do some of them have an impressive array of connectivity possibilities, but as we have seen, this is not nearly enough. Many ERP systems offer export and import facilities, which is a very poor form of integration, and maybe even does not deserve to be called integration. Some ERP systems offer some form of standardized interfacing, which is better, but still not good enough. Most ERP systems however lack coordination. Often, the claim of being well integrated means only that endpoints have been provided to which you must build your own integration solutions.

A functional application network requires vision, strategy and tactics to let its participating applications cooperate as a whole to adequately support business processes. Commonly, establishing this vision, strategy and tactics lies within the enterprise architecture team's responsibility. It is the integration architect's responsibility to see that it gets implemented in an effective, efficient and equitable manner. This means that you could argue that integration architecture merely is an aspect of enterprise architecture. On the other hand, the nature of enterprise and integration architecture differs significantly, which does justify recognition of integration architecture as a separate architecture subdomain. In a recent survey conducted in the Enterprise Architecture Network, opinions varied widely from "integration is a facet of application development" to "integration is the architecture that keeps the enterprise architecture domains consistent". Obviously, there is no shared understanding for the term. Within their context, all of the given opinions were valid. Instead of trying to find a definition of the term integration architecture, let us try to scope the term integration architecture. Within the context of this book, integration architecture comprises the transformation of an enterprise vision, strategy and tactics with regards to an applications network into making the right choices that can be programmed or configured in integration tooling.

The above statement surmises that a conceptual framework exists that addresses the fabric of the applications network, and how applications, whether home-grown or of-the-shelf, must fit into this network. In a top-down architecture approach, there is an enterprise architecture body that is responsible for defining and maintaining this conceptual framework, which is not always the case.

If the organization does not support this top-down approach, the integration architect may have to resort to a sort of bottom-up approach, also known under the term "guerilla architecture". Then it is up to the integration architect to develop the conceptual framework. This entails a piecemeal approach, by addressing the discrete business problems at hand, weaving the enterprise architecture context around them as they present themselves. It is more a "hit and run" architecture than an all-out "mobilizing an army" architecture, and in fact, a piecemeal "hit and run" architecture might succeed where an all-out approach may prove to be too large a bite. It does however require a great deal of versatility from the integration architect.

Making the wrong decisions when creating the fabric of an applications network or creating the wrong integration solutions to land on the applications network can be extremely costly. This cost must come out of the KTLO (Keep the Lights On) budget, which is often a very large portion of the total corporate IT budget. Due to dependencies within an applications network and the fractalic nature of adaptations to an applications network, it is often extremely difficult or even impossible to calculate a reliable ROI (Return-on-Investment) for these activities, especially since typically there are often little or no short-term benefits; typically the benefits show a long-term hyperbolic curve, starting low but increasing with time. In IT organizations where investment decisions are largely based on ROI or CBA (Cost/Benefit Analysis) instead of TCO (Total Cost of Ownership), it can be very difficult to obtain funding for investing in indirect, not business-driven improvements.

This book addresses establishing a vision, strategy and tactics for defining and maintaining an applications network, specifically the fabric of the network, and the fitting of applications in that network. In the end, the applications network will need to be supported by technology and tooling, but for the vision, strategy and tactics, the technology and tooling is rather irrelevant, and therefore only marginally addressed. Also rather irrelevant is whether a top-down or bottom-up approach is used, although in the latter case, support from the organization will be very helpful. What is most significant, and the main topic of this book, is the conceptual framework for the applications network, which governs how applications in the network should communicate and coordinate.

1.1 Why bother?

A holistic approach towards an applications network may sound like an academic exercise to many, but there are significant tangible and intangible benefits. Technical incidents in an IT network can never be totally avoided, but they are generally easily fixed. A collection of poorly integrated applications however can give rise to functional incidents that will be very hard and costly to fix. The approach described here will eliminate these hard-to-fix incidents by describing how to evolve from a collection of disparate applications, that each per se supports its part of the business process to an integrated applications network designed to support the whole of your business processes. The premise of the business process centric approach entails an integration layer that is modeled after business processes instead of domains or applications, and is designed to support these business processes instead of fulfilling the data needs of certain applications. This allows for a stable basis that enables agile responses to changing demands without affecting the underlying applications. Short-term benefits will be small, but in the long term, this approach will be able to dramatically lower both KTLO costs and costs of application development and integration. Simultaneously, business agility can be significantly increased and business process control can be notably improved.

1.2 Audience

Many roles can be distinguished in modern corporate IT, and this book is aimed at all roles that have some involvement with software development or software implementation. Chapters 1 thru 5 do not go too far into details, and pertain to why to use the business process centric approach in application integration. These chapters can be read by anyone with affinity with corporate IT. Chapters 6 and 7 clarify how to apply this approach, and are specifically written for software architects, designers and developers and integration architects, designers and developers. Chapter 8 delves into the tooling that could host the applications network and chapter 9 discusses the position of the integration architect in the IT organization.

1.3 Takeaways

- Data integration and application integration may share many common features, but are fundamentally different.
- Application integration is about distributing the support of business processes across various applications.
- Focus on data instead of processes and emphasis on scoped projects will lead to integration solutions that do not adequately fit business process requirements, hence will lead to potentially escalating incidents and hence are more costly (both monetary and in reputation) in the long-run.
- A holistic approach where solutions are designed upfront to integrate into an applications network to support business processes will drastically reduce incidents and incident escalation and hence is much more cost effective in the long-run.
- It's not the tool that counts, it's how you use it, and what you use it for.

Additional takeaways for the software architect, designer and builder:
- It is business processes, not data models, that require the exchange of information.
- It is business processes, not data models, that define the content of the information being exchanged.
- The choice of integration patterns is primarily governed by applications' responsibility.
- The integration pattern is more decisive for the choice of technology than the platforms involved.

2 Introduction

A lot has been written about application software integration, and indeed, many people have made invaluable contributions in this field, like Gregor Hohpe and Bobby Woolf with their work on Enterprise Integration Patterns, expanding on Erich Gamma's work on software design patterns, or David Linthicum's "Enterprise Application Integration", aging but still relevant. There are many more excellent works that concentrate on patterns and techniques to implement integration solutions. Still, in practice, many integration projects fail to deliver. In most cases this can be attributed to a focus on the technique of how to implement the flow of data. The traditional approach to application integration is to identify data requirements, then to find out where to get that data, and finally how to get and transport that data. We forget to look at the role that the flow of data plays in the whole, the whole not only being the system landscape of solutions, within which the integration solutions must fit, but more importantly, the whole also being the set of business processes that the integration solutions need to support.

> "Always design a thing by considering it in its next larger context – a chair in a room, a room in a house, a house in an environment, an environment in a city plan."
> Eliel Saarinen, architect.

Eliel Saarinen's message to consider any subject within its context, while valid for any subject, is especially important when architecting integration solutions.

When looking at incidents in integration solutions, we can differentiate them into two categories. Incidents in the first category, technical failures (like a network connection down, an expired certificate), are usually not very costly, and easily remedied. Incidents in the second category, functional failures (like data inconsistency, data semantics), are often very damaging and very difficult and costly to repair, as repeatedly demonstrated in the Standish Chaos Reports. In the end, functional failures occur when the models that you use, whether a data model, service model, or whichever model, do not correspond with the reality of our business processes. For the most part, we understand this in application development, but we tend to forget this when facing integration issues.

A tremendous amount of documents have been published on integration patterns, integration protocols, integration tooling and the software architecture of integration solutions. Some of these writings are extremely valuable, and I have added a selection to the bibliography paragraph as recommended reading material. However, by and large, they tell us how to implement the choices that were made to devise integration solutions. But much more important than how to implement these choices is the process of conceiving the appropriate integration solutions and making the right choices. The overemphasis on the technological side of integration draws our attention away from the main issue in integration architecture: there is little or no guidance available on when or why to use certain integration patterns, and how information content relates to integration patterns.

"IT doesn't matter" was the provocative title of a controversial article that Nicholas Carr published in Harvard Business Review in 2003. Nick argued that for something to be of strategic advantage it must be scarce, and since IT has become a commodity, and as such no longer offers strategic value, IT no longer matters. He did not say that we did not need IT, in fact he acknowledged that IT has become essential to support your business processes. He only said that as a strategic differentiator IT doesn't matter. This postulate "IT doesn't matter" is very applicable to integration architecture, albeit with a different interpretation.

Since 1994 the Standish group publishes the yearly Chaos Report, which reports on the success and failure rates of IT projects globally. Astonishingly, the figures remain more or less the same, year after year. It seems the IT industry does not learn from its failures. Even more astonishingly, year after year business users name the same cause as one of the main reasons for IT project failure: IT solutions fail to meet expectations. It is the solutions that IT offers, that fail to deliver, it is not the underlying technology: the technology doesn't matter. Technology is the way you may implement an integration pattern, and for this platform, or this project, or this timeframe you may choose a different technology than for the next platform, project or timeframe. What does matter is which integration patterns to use, and why, how and when to use them. This, the technology independent aspects of application integration, is what we will focus on. These basics are stable, they remain the same, irrespective of technology. Whether you use cloud services, microservices, API's, or whatever technology is currently on the hype-cycle, is irrelevant since the underlying patterns remain the same. The technology is the tooling with which you realize these patterns, and you should choose the right tools for the job, not choose the right job for the tools. The solutions count, the technology doesn't matter.

Just as in real-world architecture, the world of planning, designing, and constructing buildings and other physical structures, integration architecture is not about tooling or technology. It is about the solutions you plan, design and build with tooling and technology. The oldest known reference work on architecture, the multi-volume work "*De Architectura*" was written around 30 BC by Vitruvius, a Roman military engineer and architect. According to Vitruvius, good architecture should satisfy the three principles of *firmitas, utilitas et venustas*, or in plain English durability, functionality and elegance. The same three principles still apply today for integration architecture, but in view of rapidly business evolution, for integration architecture we should add a fourth principle: agility, the speed with which information systems can react and adapt to changes in their environment.

A plethora of publications address the technology to achieve durability and agility in integration architecture. What is missing in the field of integration architecture until now, is a set of guidelines to achieve the other two principles, functionality and elegance.

Principles are illustrated and examples are given from the perspective of the fictitious Acme Corporation, a long-standing mid-size enterprise that builds luxury cars. This fictitious enterprise is chosen for its variety and diversity in business processes, as illustrated in figure 1a.

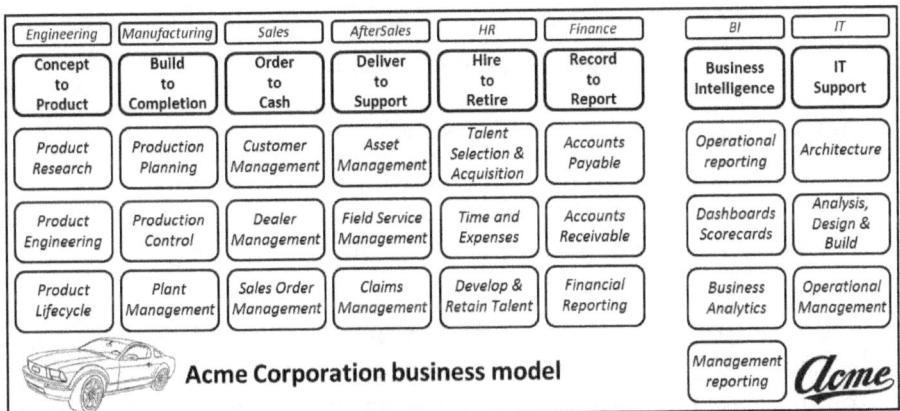

Engineering	Manufacturing	Sales	AfterSales	HR	Finance	BI	IT
Concept to Product	Build to Completion	Order to Cash	Deliver to Support	Hire to Retire	Record to Report	Business Intelligence	IT Support
Product Research	Production Planning	Customer Management	Asset Management	Talent Selection & Acquisition	Accounts Payable	Operational reporting	Architecture
Product Engineering	Production Control	Dealer Management	Field Service Management	Time and Expenses	Accounts Receivable	Dashboards Scorecards	Analysis, Design & Build
Product Lifecycle	Plant Management	Sales Order Management	Claims Management	Develop & Retain Talent	Financial Reporting	Business Analytics	Operational Management
		Acme Corporation business model				Management reporting	Acme

Figure 1a: Acme Corporation simplified business model

Acme was an early adopter of automation, and started building its own software to alleviate bottlenecks in various business processes in the mid 70'ies. By the end of the 80'ies Acme had most of its processes covered with in-house developed, purpose-built applications. Many of the primary business processes are still supported by these ancient homegrown applications. Of course the business processes have evolved in the last 40 years, think of engine software and other in-car software, new production techniques, more componentization, regulatory compliance. All of this has led to many adaptations, either retrofitting the changes into the existing legacy software, developing new solutions in-house, or buying and implementing commercially available solutions. The result is a quilt of disparate and disjointed applications, as shown in figure 1b.

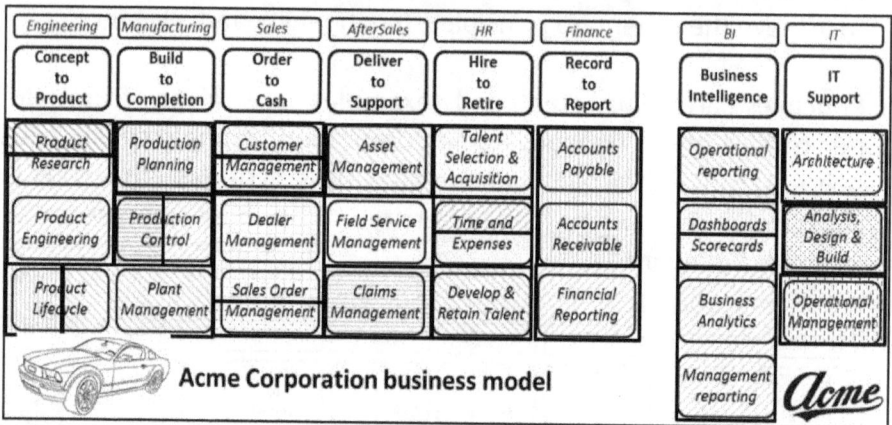

Engineering	Manufacturing	Sales	AfterSales	HR	Finance		BI	IT
Concept to Product	Build to Completion	Order to Cash	Deliver to Support	Hire to Retire	Record to Report		Business Intelligence	IT Support
Product Research	Production Planning	Customer Management	Asset Management	Talent Selection & Acquisition	Accounts Payable		Operational reporting	Architecture
Product Engineering	Production Control	Dealer Management	Field Service Management	Time and Expenses	Accounts Receivable		Dashboards Scorecards	Analysis, Design & Build
Product Lifecycle	Plant Management	Sales Order Management	Claims Management	Develop & Retain Talent	Financial Reporting		Business Analytics	Operational Management
Acme Corporation business model							Management reporting	*acme*

Figure 1b: Application coverage of business processes

About a third of ACME's applications date back from the 70'ies and 80'ies, running on a mainframe, another third are various homegrown applications written on the MS-DOS / Windows platform, varying from legacy Clipper and Visual Basic to contemporary Java and .Net. The last third is composed of commercial ERP systems. The challenge that Acme's IT department is facing is that much of the existing integration solutions are based on the export/import principle, which is increasingly impeding scale-ups, scale-outs and agility. Another challenge is that Acme's IT department needs of a lot of "tribal knowledge", local expertise and effort of an ageing workforce just to keep things running, which strains the ability to adequately respond to continuously changing demands in an ever faster evolving market. These are the fundamental challenges that give rise to many more derived challenges, such as how to replace legacy systems that cannot meet current demands without severely disrupting business processes, or how to meet or even anticipate market demands before being overtaken by the next wave of market demands.

3 History

Before automation, all business processes were executed by people. They were executed directly by people, or by machines operated by people, and the administration of the processes was registered by people. The use of computers in support of business processes took off some 50 years ago. At first, the execution of the business processes remained with people, only some calculations and the manual registration on paper was replaced by calculations and registration on tape or disk. The most used mainframe at the time, between 1965 and 1978, was the IBM System/360, with an internal memory between 256 and 1024 KB. Data was stored on tapes or disks (the 2311 disk had a capacity of 7.2 MB) and the user interface was implemented with punch cards. The first programs to run on these systems would support a tiny piece of the business processes, like order entry or payment tapes. These early programs were batch oriented, and they ran in isolation, e.g. they did not communicate with users or other programs; there were no interfaces except for the operator to load, start, stop and unload tapes and programs. Data could be shared between batch programs by accessing the same data storage. Programs were not designed to execute business processes, they were designed to register and process data.

With the introduction of alternative hardware platforms and a variety of OLTP (On-Line Transaction Processing) monitors and databases in the 70ies and 80ies, we saw the emergence of heterogeneous systems, each supporting a small piece of the business processes. An increasing number of applications and data stores that were originally developed as stand-alone solutions, needed to share their data with others. In those days, the focus of these integrations was on the data, not the process, and there really were only two ways to do this: either share the data source(s) directly, or extract data from one application or data store on a regular or incidental basis, and import it into another. In the batch-oriented environments of those early days, these were efficient and effective ways to implement data integration between applications.

In these last 50 years, application development has seen a tremendous evolution from entering pure machine code to symbolic assembly to COBOL to "Goto-Less" to "4GL". From there we progressed through structured programming and procedural programming to n-tier architecture. Object-orientation was next, followed by Model Driven Architecture and Data Driven Architecture just before the turn of the century. Service oriented architecture and event-driven architecture have gained attention in the new millennium.

These technology oriented developments are the consequence of an underlying, less obvious development. Whereas the first automated systems were meant to replace the existing manual administration of business processes, we gradually started producing automated systems that are actively supporting existing business processes. The newest technologies are especially suited to support evolution or even radical change of business processes: we want to embrace the agile business.

Somewhere between the first automation attempts and modern IT we have evolved from digital registration of business processes executed by people to the execution of business processes by applications managed by people. This is a profound difference that we are rarely aware of. You might call it an invisible revolution. It is probably the most important reason why integration of legacy systems into a modern applications network fails so often: we are trying to mesh legacy that is aimed at registering data into an applications network that is aimed to attend or execute business processes.

One of the consequences of the evolution in software development is that many organizations now have a variety of systems on various platforms under diverse operating systems in different stages of evolutionary progress (legacy versus state-of-the-art software). This is often referred to as "distributed systems". What is often forgotten is that there is a very profound dichotomy between distributed systems that are designed in that way, and distributed systems as collections of disparate applications. In the first category, the participating systems are engineered upfront to cooperate. In the second category we need to finds ways to let the participating systems cooperate afterwards: this has become the field of enterprise application integration.

Unfortunately, the evolution of application integration has not been able to keep pace with the progress in technology. In the early years, as we already saw, application integration meant transferring data from one system or application to another. It was primarily aimed at connectivity between applications, and mainly discussed communication protocols. The paradigms of the last decade, service oriented architecture and event-driven architecture, when understood and implemented correctly, implicitly address the aspects of application integration. But for organizations that have not embraced service oriented architecture or event-driven architecture, or haven't understood it, application integration is still about transferring data from one application or system to another; they still extract data from one application or data store to import it into another. They may use modern technology, modern tools and modern protocols to transport the data, but the underlying paradigm hasn't evolved.

With Model Driven Architecture, which is the fad of the day, we create various models of a target system. The extent of these models is defined by the scope of the target system, and application integration - by its nature - lies on and over the edge of this scope. If you are not fully aware of this, you risk designing isolated solutions that have to be fitted together afterwards. It tends to reduce application integration to the conciliation between the various models. It tends to reduce application integration to the transport of data between applications.

3.1 Architecture in IT

The analogy between software design and architecture was first drawn by Dijkstra in the 60ies of the previous century, but we had to wait till 1996 for the first publication that actually used the term 'software architecture': "Software Architecture: Perspectives on an Emerging Discipline" by Mary Shaw and David Garlan. In the same year Gartner coined the acronym SOA for Service Oriented Architecture but failed to define it. This has led to a complete lack of shared understanding of the acronym SOA, and everyone creating their own definitions, where the only common denominator seems to be integration trough services. Since integration can be considered a service, we can argue that Integration Architecture equals Service Oriented Architecture.

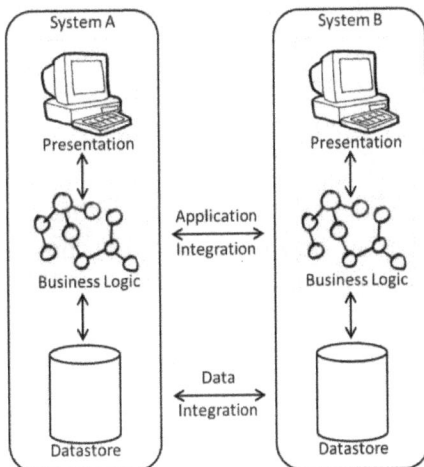

Figure 2a: Data Integration vs Application Integration

In the last decade of the previous century, three-tier architecture, which advocates physically separating presentation, business logic and data management functions, started to find a firm foothold. It is only since this century that we realized the consequences in integration architecture, and the importance of the distinction between data integration and application integration. Figure 2a represents the early view on distinguishing between data integration and application integration.

In this model, data Integration is about synchronizing data between different datastores and targets. It involves reconciliation, data manipulation, de-duplication, cleansing, standardization and other data-intensive operations. It forms a layer of abstraction over the underlying datastores. Data Integration does not concern business process support, at least not implicitly and not directly. As such, a Data Integration task might run in "batch mode" or scheduled operation once a week, once a day, once an hour, or a few times an hour, or even more often than that. It doesn't run hundreds or thousands of times an hour, though. A Data Integration task might involve a single record of data or terabytes of data.

Also in this model, application integration is about the exchange of data between applications, not data stores. It operates (near) real-time, reliably following the pace of the business processes they support. As such, it forms an abstraction level over the underlying applications and business processes. Since most business processes typically are event oriented, the amount of data involved is usually quite small.

While the distinction between data and application integration did constitute an improvement, it did not dissolve barriers between siloed systems, it merely crosses them. The next step, incorporating the three tier concept into integration solutions, makes these barriers less apparent.

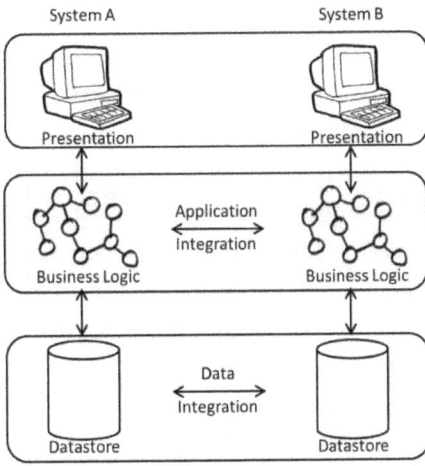

Figure 2b: Data Integration vs Application Integration

In figure 2b, data integration is placed in the data tier and application integration is placed in the business logic tier. However, it still represents exchanging data at two levels, the business logic level and datastore level, and it still does not represent what we try to achieve: integrated business process support across the business logic level. It does however clearly make the distinction between integration at the data level and integration at the application level.

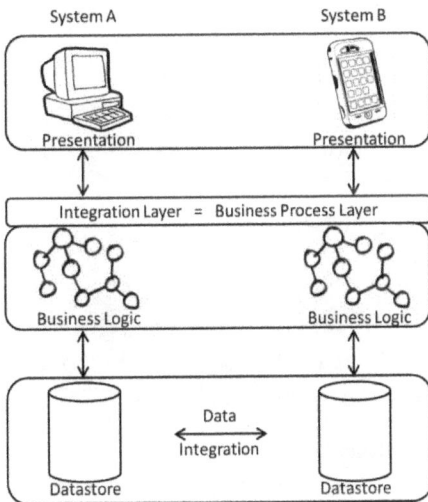

Figure 2c: Data Integration vs Application Integration

It was the concept of Service Oriented architecture (SOA) that introduced an integration layer on top of the business logic layer which contains all business services and business functions. This concept allowed us to truly remove the barriers between siloed systems, at least for the clients of the integration layer. The services and functions in this integration layer access the underlying business logic across the various applications, systems and platforms. If done correctly, they are modeled after business processes, and form an abstraction level over the underlying business logic hosted by the various applications, systems and platforms, thus allowing us to equate the term "Application Integration Layer" to the term "Business Process Layer". In this model, application integration is no longer about exchanging data between systems. Instead, it is about the support of business processes across various applications, systems and platforms. For this, process related information needs to be accessed across these various applications, systems and platforms.

SOA

Alexander Pasik, a former analyst at Gartner, is credited to have coined the term service oriented architecture in 1994. In his view, the term "client/server" had too much of a physical hardware connotation, and he used SOA to describe a "client software/server software" architecture. The term did not gain momentum until in 2000 web services were introduced, first by Microsoft, soon followed by all other major vendors, since the hype was now created. This led to many believing SOA and web services to be the same, and a panacea for every conceivable issue in IT.
In 2002 it was Gartner again to popularize the term ESB in 2002, and again the hype caught on, and all major and many minor vendors hurried to rebrand their message broking solutions as ESB. Soon, an ESB was considered to be a mandatory foundation for SOA.

While there is much agreement on what capabilities a SOA and ESB should display, there is little agreement on the SOA and ESB concepts as a whole. To end an ongoing debate about what is or isn't SOA, a manifesto was published in 2009. This manifesto listed six core values of SOA as follows:

1.   Business value over technical strategy
2.   Strategic goals over project-specific benefits
3.   Intrinsic interoperability over custom integration
4.   Shared services over specific-purpose implementations
5.   Flexibility over optimization

6.   Evolutionary refinement over pursuit of initial perfection

Although the first two core values stress the importance of business value and strategic goals, the whole set of suggested core values is quite technically oriented. Herein lies the core of the problem with SOA; it is almost always considered from a technological viewpoint. The manifesto failed to mention that the first two values aren't just guidelines, they are the foundations without which a SOA cannot exist.

Most commonly, SOA is defined as a list of capabilities. But just like a collection of car parts is not a car, a collection of capabilities does not constitute a SOA. Even a carefully selected collection of cooperating capabilities may not constitute a SOA. Most of all SOA is a strategy, a strategy that can be implemented with a variety of architectures and a range of technologies.

Pulling event driven architecture (EDA) into service oriented architecture to form what was briefly known as SOA 2.0 clearly shows the positioning of SOA in the business process layer. Unfortunately, many did not understand the tight relationship between SOA and business processes, which led to many failures of projects that sought to adopt it and gave SOA its undeserved bad reputation.

4   The Problem Space

Nowadays monolithic systems running on a single central processor have by and large made way for collections of applications and systems, that may run on different hardware, operating systems and platforms. Sometimes such a collection of applications is called distributed system. The term is somewhat ambiguous: basically, you can divide distributed systems up into two main categories: the first category is formed by the systems that are designed to be distributed: fine examples are client-server systems, three-tier and n-tier systems, peer-to-peer systems. Integration is an important aspect in this category, and the ideas presented here are very much applicable to this category, and can be implemented within these systems.

The second category is formed by the collections of applications and systems that are not distributed by design; instead they happen to run on different hardware, operating systems and platforms. For this category, integration is mostly added as separate solutions outside these systems. It is this category where integration solutions become problematic and where the ideas presented here are most significant.

IT projects of the first generation did not much more than replacing manual registration of information by automated registration. Obviously, the attention was heavily geared towards the data being registered, not towards the processes that are involved. For most IT departments this is still the case. This is clearly demonstrated be the fact that the jobtitles "information analyst" and "data analyst" are ubiquitous in IT departments all over the world, but the jobtitle "process analyst" is rarely represented in an IT department. Unsurprisingly, traditional integration solutions are heavily geared towards integration of data.

With the silent revolution towards application networks executing the business processes the traditional data integration approach is no longer viable. The support of primary business processes requires an application network based on business process centric application integration to offer the necessary cooperation, coordination and organization.

While unavoidably there are many similarities between data integration and application integration, like standardization, transformation, reconciliation, communication to name a few, the differences are essential. Typically, these capabilities are supplied in an "Integration Platform", which can be anything from a vendor supplied all-encompassing solution, to a collection of diverse tools that can cooperate to provide these capabilities. The similarities between data and application integration may warrant to uphold one integration platform to support both types. The differences however are so fundamental that they justify for both types to have their own platform: a data integration platform and an application integration platform. Both approaches have their pros and cons.

Data integration is typically used in ETL processes for data warehousing and business intelligence environments, whereas application integration is typically used in operational environments for primary business process support. Before the general adoption of three-tier architecture, the distinction between data integration and application integration was not made, and integration took place on the datastore level. These integrations would be based on different models:

- Physical data models: These are the hardest models to integrate. For reconciliation of physical data models you need specialist knowledge of both models, preferably combines in one person. Potential reuse of these integrations is practically zero.

- Logical data models: Logical data models are easier to reconcile, and stand a much better chance of being reused. However, often logical data models are an (almost) 1:1 reflection of the physical data models; in that case, the same observations as for physical data models apply.
- Domain models: domain models are conceptual frameworks of a domain that incorporate both data and behavior. Unfortunately, in practice domain models concentrate heavily or even solely on logical data models, and often neglect or even ignore the dynamic behavioral aspects. Business process modeling is as much if not more pertinent to domain models. If business process models are not at the base of your integration design, domain model based integration offers no benefits over logical data model based integration.

A typical data integration pattern is the data replication pattern; one possible implementation involves scheduling the creation of a datastore extraction, and export it as a file for one or more clients to be imported by them. Another possible implementation is to collect and send delta's (for example, data that has a *"LastModified"* timestamp that is later than the last delta collection). In the days before we knew three-tiered architectures, and before we understood the essential difference between data integration and application integration, these integration implementations were common. Nowadays security demands, business agility and service orientation, not to mention cloud services, internet-of-things and regulatory compliance invalidate the traditional data integration approach for primary business processes.

As traditional approaches are becoming untenable, in an environment where business agility is increasingly important, making the distinction between data integration and application integration has become essential. Not making this distinction and applying traditional data integration patterns where application integration patterns are called for, will lead to consequences:

- Clients don't get the information they should have: even if the data content reflects all the required information, when exchanging data extractions you will lose the business context of the data. You don't know what business processes and events have led to the data.
- Clients get information they do not want: full data extractions by definition are redundant, since they send the same data over and over again. But delta extractions often also are redundant, since due to lack of business process or event context, they will send any and all changes, also those you aren't interested in.
- Clients get the data too late: If, for whatever reason, a scheduled dataset is not delivered in time, dependent scheduled processes will fail, or produce faulty output.
- Clients get the data too early: data that is received too early gets discarded or needs to be stored for processing at a more convenient moment.
- Clients may need to reconstruct (business) events: since you cannot know what business processes and events have led to the data, business events need to be reconstructed based on differences between the current extraction and the previous extraction. For example, the introduction of a new product line may only become apparent when noticing a product line in your extraction that didn't exist in the previous extraction.
- Clients risk data inconsistency: Since the data models differ, so will the restrictions within the data models differ. This will often lead to data inconsistency, or with data validation or data cleansing in place, to missing data.
- Sources risk limited or no reusability: data integrations are often designed to meet requirements of the client; these are

often specific enough as to become unusable for other prospective clients. For these clients a similar, but slightly different data integrations will need to be created, which leads to redundancy.

- Sources risk redundancy: clients with similar, but slightly different requirements will need similar, but slightly different integration solutions.
- Solutions risk lack of business process fit: As an example: hardware components and software components are both components of a car. Traditional replication based integration methods would send hardware and software component information simultaneously. The fact that the associated business processes are totally different (software component changes for physical cars are sent *from* the factory *to* a workshop for many cars at a time, whereas hardware component changes on a physical car are sent *from* a workshop *to* the factory for a single car) require that they should be exchanged separately.
- Solutions risk lack of business process agility: Since the business processes are not reflected as integration services that are ready to be used as recombinable building blocks, business process rules are caught inside source code, where they generally can be changed only through large effort, cost, and impact.

Within any organization that has to cope with legacy systems, all of the above issues will have occurred in the past, some frequently, some less frequent, some costly, some less costly, and they will continue to occur in the future if the issues are not addressed.

At the other end of the spectrum, we see new technologies emerging, which is a natural process, to be expected in complex adaptive environments such as information technology. We also are getting overwhelmed by waves of publicity around new developments, whether they really represent innovative ideas or technologies, or just are rebranding old ones. The common pattern of initial enthusiasm, adoption and disillusionment induced the IT research and advisory firm Gartner to create their hype-cycle model to describe this pattern. Ironically, Gartner itself is at the basis of several hype cycles.

Adoption of these hyped ideas *per se* (a.k.a. *jumping on the bandwagon*) is always ill-advised. In almost every case, the initial idea is sound and solid, but incorrect application of the idea causes failure and disillusionment. Just as a craftsman does not select a tool to then decide what to build with it, so too one should not adopt a novel technology, idea or concept, then decide where to apply it.

Instead, the new developments in technology should be carefully studied and understood. In almost every case you will notice that either you are already doing it, or that it is merely an addition to your existing capabilities and you can fit it into your existing architecture.

This book seeks to provide sufficient background information on integration architecture to allow better evaluation of new developments, and enable well-founded decisions if these new developments would extend or enhance your applications network with new or better capabilities, and if they do, when and how to fit them into the fabric of your existing applications network.

5   The Solution Space

> Application integration is the set of services that enable
> the integration of applications across an enterprise.
> Modified after Wikipedia

According to Wikipedia, application integration is a middleware framework composed of a collection of technologies and services which enable integration of systems and applications across an enterprise. This definition is widely adopted, but it suggests that application integration belongs in the realm of technology. This misconception often leads to obscure integration solutions that *per se* may be well constructed and well performing, but as part of a system landscape perform poorly, cause many an incident, and require too much maintenance.

> ACME wants to offer its customers a choice of extended support on its sold cars: they should be able to choose between three levels of support: bronze, silver or gold. ACME will have to register the support level for each customer, and it has several options to do so. It could be done within the existing CRM solution, it could also be done within the existing support management solution, ACME could develop a custom solution, and maybe there are other solutions that could host this functionality. This is obviously an integration issue in which an integration architect must be involved: how do you integrate the desired functionality into the existing applications network?

The erroneous perception that integration is no more than an exchange of data may cause software development teams to design software without attention to how it collaborates and harmonizes with other software. Integration is designed as data transfer solutions without attention to three of the pillars of integration:

shared understanding, coordination and organization. Sometimes an integration specialist is called in to implement the technology needed to exchange data between the applications that are involved. This phenomenon is called "integration as an afterthought" and, sadly, it is common practice.

IT enterprise applications or systems have just one goal, and that is the support of business processes. As business processes are often supported by various enterprise applications or systems (as in figure 1b), we must make sure these enterprise applications or systems cooperate. With this in mind, we can redefine integration as the support of business processes across various applications or systems.

> Application integration is the support of business
> processes across various applications or systems.

Let us state this assertion very explicitly again: there is only one reason to build or buy enterprise application software: we buy or build enterprise application software to support our business processes. IT people tend to forget this; they tend to design and build enterprise application software to fulfill a model; they tend to see the development, maintenance and management of application software as a goal unto itself.

> We build or buy enterprise application software to
> support business processes.

This assertion has some far-reaching consequences. First of all, it implies that you need to know your business processes; how else can you decide if your application software is supporting your business processes? Second, while process control software supports the processes themselves, enterprise application software above all supports the information flow in your processes.

> Application integration is the implementation of the business process information flows between applications or systems.

Third, your applications and systems form the constituting parts of the system landscape that is supporting your business processes. If we extrapolate the axioma *"It's better to have a system of poorly optimized parts that cooperate smoothly than a system of highly optimized parts that cooperate poorly."*, then it follows that good application integration is more important than the applications themselves. It also says your system landscape must not be a haphazard collection of applications, but a carefully constructed network of applications.

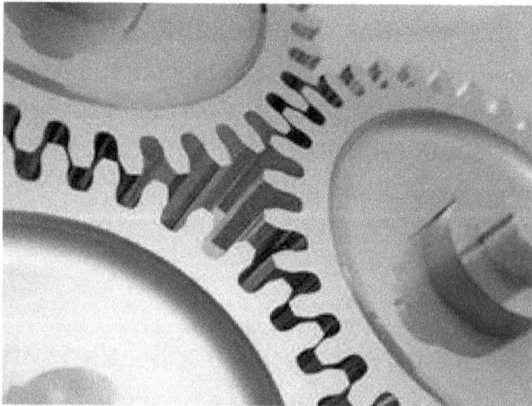

Figure 3: *"It's better to have a system of poorly optimized parts that cooperate smoothly than a system of highly optimized parts that cooperate poorly."*

Hence fourth, application integration should not be an afterthought, the conciliation and transport of data between various models, but should be a forethought, the models being based on the information flows between the business processes.

Fifth, the whole of your system landscape supports the whole of your (and maybe some of your business partner's) business processes; this makes it a system of systems, which inevitably is non-linear, and does not respond well to the traditional top-down approaches. Instead, studying systems of systems will require a systemic approach, combining top-down and bottom-up methods with analytical and synthetical thinking.

Reasoning along this line-of-thought inevitably brings us to the conclusion that effective integration is not about exchanging data between applications; it's goal is much more fundamental:

> **Application integration is the support of your business processes across heterogeneous and disparate applications and platforms.**

5.1 Systems of systems

The "classical" or Cartesian (named after Rene Descartes, 1596-1650) mode of thinking, expressed most explicitly in Newtonian mechanics, dominated the scientific worldview until the beginning of the 20th century. It is based on the following assumptions:
- aristotelian logic: a phenomenon belongs either to category "A", or to "not A". It cannot be both, neither, in between, or "it depends".

- reductionism or analysis: to fully understand a system you decompose it into its constituent elements and their fundamental properties.
- determinism: every change can be represented as a trajectory of the system through (state) space, i.e. a linear sequence of states, following fixed laws of nature. These laws completely determine the trajectory towards the future (predictability) as well as towards the past (reversibility) .

The classic view of determinism was expressed by Pierre-Simon Laplace (1749 – 1827) in his postulation that, given sufficient knowledge of every particle in the universe, any future or past event could be calculated with exactitude. This postulation is known as "Laplace's demon". Determinism is closely related to reductionism. Reductionism says that complex 'wholes' can be understood through knowledge of its simpler, constituent parts. Conversely, it implies that knowledge of its parts leads to understanding the whole. Reductionism tells us that any inability to predict more than probabilities is simply due to ignorance.

Beginning of the 20th century, pioneers in various fields of sciences started looking beyond the limits of the old paradigms, and new models were proposed. Ongoing discoveries of the limitations of linear causation thinking moved these fields into the next step – "systemic causation" models. In these models, the very presence of the observer influences the field. Here, feedback loops and feed forward loops added new complications and complexities to our understanding about how things actually work. It brought to our awareness that the effects, results, and products of a previous cause can, and frequently will, enter back into the system itself as a cause of yet another effect. Now we no longer have cause-and-effect, we have cause-effect-cause-effect-cause-etc. When Edward Lorenz described this in 1963 for the first time in his paper "Deterministic

Nonperiodic Flow", he opened up a whole new field of science: Complexity Science.

5.2 Complexity

A complex system is a group of interdependent parts that function as a whole. The key words in this phrase are "complex" and "interdependent". First we must understand that complex and complicated are not the same. Sending a man to set foot on the moon is a very complicated mission, but it is not complex. On the other hand, the machinations on the stock exchange markets are very complex, but not at all complicated. Complexity is caused by the interdependent character of the relationship between constituent parts of a system. A change in a part influences the whole, but if this change also influences other parts, which in turn influence the whole too, amplifying or dampening each other, the net result can be anything between no difference at all and an out-of-control run-away train of change, the latter option better known as "the butterfly effect". In fact, the net result of a change anywhere in any complex systems is unpredictable.

The term "butterfly effect" was originally coined in 1963 by Edward Lorenz to illustrate the example where minor perturbations such as the flapping of the wings of a butterfly may catalyze the formation of a tornado. Indeed, weather patterns remain one of the best examples in complexity science. Clearly, the weather is governed by totally deterministic physics laws. Our understanding of these deterministic physics laws permit us to predict the weather in the short term, yet the interdependency of the net results of these laws induce a complexity that makes the weather totally unpredictable in the long term. Once meteorologists realized that a deterministic approach could not bring the desired results, they found that studying the weather at a higher abstraction level, that of weather patterns, offered better results in weather prediction.

System or application integration is about integrating systems or applications into larger systems or applications. As we have seen, the complexity of the resulting system will depend on the degree of interdependency in the integrations. If a system has no interdependent parts then it may be complicated, but it's not complex. The degree of interdependency between the parts determines the degree of complexity of the whole: in fact complexity will increase exponentially with increasing interdependency. It is therefore of the utmost importance to keep the degree of interdependency in integrations as low as possible.

The real reason to avoid point-to-point integration.

We all know the drawings of spaghetti integration where a number of applications, all communicating directly with each other. The number of connections is determined by the formula $n * (n - 1) / 2$ where n is the number of applications involved, and this is then postulated as a compelling reason to adopt a hub-and-spoke model or a bus model. It's not true.

Let's have a look at general systems theory. A system is a group of parts that function as a whole. In other words, there is a dependency between a system and its constituent parts. An interdependency occurs when a part of a system influences another part of that system. For example: if a change in part A cause a change in part B, and this causes a change again in part A, then we have a system with two interdependent parts, where the eventual effect on the system of a change in one of the parts will be unpredictable. These systems with interdependent parts are called complex adaptive systems (CAS), and they are the subject of study of complexity science (a.k.a. Chaos Theory).

Theoretically, the complexity of a CAS can be calculated. In a system where all parts are fully interdependent, the complexity index formula is n!-1 (n-faculty minus 1). However, interdependency is not a discrete attribute (yes or no), it is a degree from 0% to 100%. Taking this into

---

account, the complexity index formula would be **(n^d)!-1** where d is the degree (0 to 1).

Parts n	Connections n*(n-1)/2	Complexity n!-1	Complexity (n^d)!-1 for d = 0.5
2	1	1	0.41
3	3	5	1.45
4	6	26	2.89
5	10	119	9.85
6	15	719	25.83
7	21	5039	69.99
8	28	40319	199.79
9	36	362879	601.39
10	45	3628799	1903.94

The table shows the number of connections and the calculated complexity index of systems consisting of 2 to 10 parts. Whereas the number of connections increases progressively, the complexity index really explodes. Point-to-point connections are dependencies that show interdependent behavior to a degree. They fall into the fourth column. Obviously, interdependency is a far more important factor than the number of connections. Reducing complexity is the real reason to avoid point-to-point integration.

5.3   Loose coupling

The technique we use to keep interdependencies in integrations as low as possible is called loose coupling. Two subjects are highly loose-coupled if they have a high degree of autonomy. Loose coupling is aimed at maximizing autonomy and minimizing interdependencies.

autonomy	components	how
reference	don't know each other	use logical addresses
time	execute at their own pace	use asynchronous protocols through queueing
format	may use different formats of data exchanged	adhere to Standards / use mediation
platform	may work in different environments, written in different languages	use standard protocols

Table 1: Achieve loose coupling through autonomy of components

We can achieve loose coupling by minimizing the number of interdependencies and by minimizing the impact of interdependencies. One of most basic patterns to implement loose coupling is layering, and a well-known example of this is the "3-Tier Architecture" pattern, which tells us to divide our applications into DAL (Data Access Layer), BL (Business Logic) and PL (Presentation Layer). This is also called horizontal layering, and it is a good example of technical loose coupling. In fact, one might say that any design pattern in programming supports the notion of technical loose coupling. It is also a good example of the first principle of addressing complexity: exchange interdependencies for simple dependencies which are much less harmful. In the case of a simple dependency, the dependent object (the *depender*) cannot change its dependency at will. The object that is depended on (the *dependee*) however can change the dependency, and its dependers will have to follow.

An obvious way to substitute dependencies for interdependencies is to *Split and Combine* on a functional basis into a hierarchy of components without circular references. In the hierarchy, we make sure that child components are only dependent on their parent, not on any sibling or child. This approach is based on sound software architecture principles, but one pitfall must be avoided. Loose-coupling becomes increasingly important in the higher levels of the hierarchy of components, but climbing the hierarchy of components means leaving the domain of software architecture and entering the domain of business architecture. Componentization that seems sensible from a software architecture point of view may well be pointless from a business architecture point of view. See also figure 5.

Introducing a level of indirection is one of the most powerful methods to handle complex or complicated issues. At run-time, this can be realized by introducing a *Mediator*, for example a *message broker* or *message bus*; at design-time invariant active or passive levels of decoupling can be introduced. You can do this by introducing a *Controller* that determines the behavior (active) or structure (passive) of the components it controls. An example of active decoupling is the separation of execution and control, where one component controls the behavior of a set of executing components. Examples of passive decoupling are adopting a standard, contract-first development, policy compliance.

All of the above patterns are very well known and well documented, but not in terms of (inter)dependency. If these patterns are implemented without giving interdependency reduction the sufficient attention, chances are that you will still end up with complex and uncontrollable solutions.

The term horizontal layering suggests that there is something like vertical layering. Vertical layering is loose coupling on a functional level by honoring functional cohesion and ensuring separation of concerns is also known as vertical layering. The problem here, again, is that the terms "cohesion" and "separation of concerns" are invariably associated with programming techniques, which is a very restrictive, technology oriented view. With vertical layering we aim for integration solutions that have one single, independent functional purpose, and all data involved must pertain to that one single, independent functional purpose. The distinction between vertical layering and stovepiping is vital, but can sometimes be quite delicate: vertical layering involves functional boundaries, which is good, stovepiping involves organizational boundaries, which is bad.

Tight and Loose coupling.

Contrary to what many believe, the term "Loose coupling" does not stem from object oriented programming. The term was first coined by Karl E. Weick in 1976, when publishing "Educational Organizations as Loosely Coupled Systems" where he describes how organizations can survive in rapidly changing environments. Fifteen years later, the term was adopted so successfully in object oriented programming that nowadays many associate loose coupling with OOP.

Dan Foody's definition*) nails the essence of loose coupling: "The state in which the impact of change (change in consumers, providers, or cross-cutting policies) is minimized across dependencies."

Tight coupling involves interdependency, and loose coupling is all about avoiding interdependency. In a previous post I demonstrated the unescapable relation between complexity and interdependency. If you have interdependencies, you have complexity: it's a mathematical law. It clearly shows that a little less tight coupling immediately will lead to a dramatic drop in complexity. Reducing complexity therefore is the most important reason to adopt loose coupling.

This is not specific to programming, it is pervasive throughout any system, be it populations, eco-systems, evolution, traffic, a living cell, weather, legislation, or any other system: the degree of interdependency (or degree of coupling) determines the complexity of that system. That is why loose coupling on application level, business process level and even organizational level is orders of magnitude more important that on programming level.

*) Designing service interfaces, Dan Foody, 2005

39

Service composition is not tight coupling: on the contrary, we create autonomous, independent services so we can use them as building blocks. It allows you to combine independent smaller services into larger, more encompassing services, that can act as larger building blocks.

Loosely coupled integration.

If you google the term "Loose coupling", you will be overwhelmed with pages that explain the technicalities of loose coupling, how to achieve it in which language using which pattern, using what tooling, which protocols etc. . . We tend to totally disregard the functional side of tight and loose coupling.

Let's consider a situation we all know. A Boolean variable can be represented in various ways: Yes or No, true or false, 1 or 0 (this latter one is especially pernicious, since in some programming languages 0 signifies true, and 1 signifies false!). Now if you want to exchange information between applications, and you need to know of each of these applications how they implement their Boolean variables, then no amount of technical loose coupling can hide the fact that you still have an interdependency on the content of your information.

To mitigate these interdependencies on information content we create canonical data models, standardized "intermediate" representations of the information. The problem is, good canonical models are extremely hard to create. A good canonical model needs to be stable, versatile and encompassing. These very challenging requirements will inevitably lead to highly abstract and often voluminous data models, which tend to be hard to understand. As they also need to be devoid of local implementation details, by consequence, these canonical models will have a hard time finding acceptance within the organization.

In view of all this, one might conclude that creating canonical models isn't worth that much effort. However, the reverse is true: technical loose coupling isn't worth doing without the use of canonical models. Reducing

---

technical dependencies without reducing functional dependencies is a waste of time.

Notice that batch processing is also a form of tight coupling: it tightly couples instances that otherwise would be independent and autonomous.

ACME has a production line where cars are built to order. each day. To assist this, ACME has a production planning system that runs a daily batch process to plan the sequence in which these cars will be built. This batch run also creates the workorderinstructions for each car. ACME would like to be able to intervene in the planning to insert a high-priority build into the planned sequence. In principle, the planned sequence could be suspended, the new car inserted, and the normal sequence could be resumed again. But here is the problem: for the new car a workorderinstruction is needed, and the existing solution does not allow to create a workorderinstruction for a single car. Rerunning the entire batch process would produce a new but unviable planning. Rerunning the batch process for the remainder of the cars was never foreseen.

This example illustrates two forms of functional tight-coupling: the planning and the workorderinstruction functions are coupled, where they should be autonomous functions, and the creation of workorderinstructions are coupled in one batch where in reality they have no mutual dependency whatsoever.

5.4 The systemic approach

The study of complex systems requires a different approach. Analytical thinking is the way of thinking that we are trained to do. We isolate a problem, and analyze it. If it's still too complicated, we divide it up into smaller parts, then analyze the parts. This typically characterizes the top-down approach, descending into more detail. Analytical thinking is intended to deal with complicated systems, not complex systems; it works fine for Newtonian mechanics, for deterministic, predictable systems. By itself, it doesn't work for complex systems.

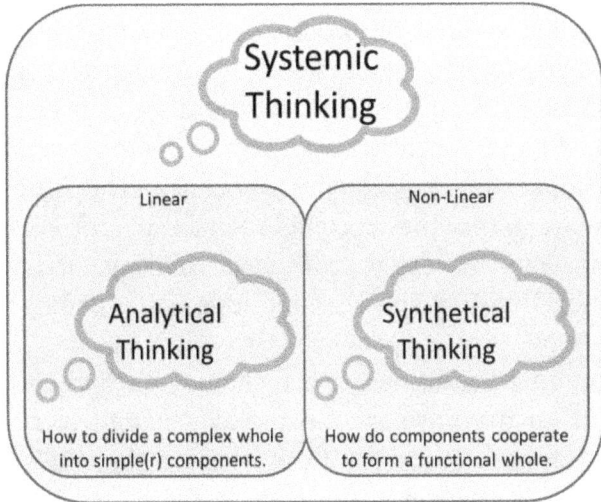

Figure 4: Systemic thinking

Synthetical thinking concentrates on understanding how constituent parts integrate to form a working a system. Up to a certain level we often unconsciously use synthetical thinking. However, when conscious analysis and unconscious synthesis do not provide results, we do not consciously choose for synthetic thinking, but tend to analyze further and deeper, which, for complex systems, produces no results and more than often ends in "analysis paralysis". Consciously choosing for synthetical thinking when studying complex systems will deliver better results. Synthetical thinking is intended to deal with complex systems; it is the bottom-up approach, synthesis into higher levels. In this sense, synthesis is the integration of constituent parts to form a functioning whole; this is what IT integration is about.

Integration is about the synthesis of constituent parts to form a functioning whole.

To really understand systems of systems, analytical thinking is not enough, it requires synthetical thinking too. Analytical (linear) thinking and synthetical (non-linear) thinking are complementary. When studying complex systems, an analytical approach without synthetical thinking produces incoherence and disconnection. On the other hand, a synthetical approach without analytical thinking will produce vagueness and ambiguity. The study of complex systems requires the correct balance of the two, consciously knowing when to apply synthetical thinking, and when to apply synthetical thinking. The systemic approach is finding this balance.

For integration solutions, the technique to find this balance is to break down the business functionalities until you have identified atomic business processes (ABP's). Once the ABP's are identified, you assemble them into business scenarios. So what exactly is an atomic business process. Surprisingly, there is no formal definition of the term. An informal definition might be "the lowest-level process that makes sense to the business". Atomic in this sense does not mean it cannot be a composite of smaller processes, it means that dividing into smaller processes makes no sense from a business point of view. A classic example is a money transfer transaction. Technically, you may have a composition of two (or more) sub-processes, one to debit the source account and one to credit the target account. From a business point of view, recognizing these as separate sub-processes makes no sense, since businesswise they cannot exist separately.

From an IT point of view we can translate the tentative definition of an ABP from above as "the lowest-level process that we want to expose as a business service". In the decomposition phase of the business process modelling effort, you iteratively descend from higher level to lower level processes. Each iteration consists of an analysis phase, where you analyze the higher level process and subdivide into lower level processes, and a synthesis phase, where you fine-tune the lower level processes so they cooperate smoothly to support the higher level process. For each business process, whether it be high level, low level or atomic, the flow of information involved in the process is defined, business triggers and events are identified, and the requirements with respect to the information flow are established. You repeat this until you have reached the level of atomic business processes.

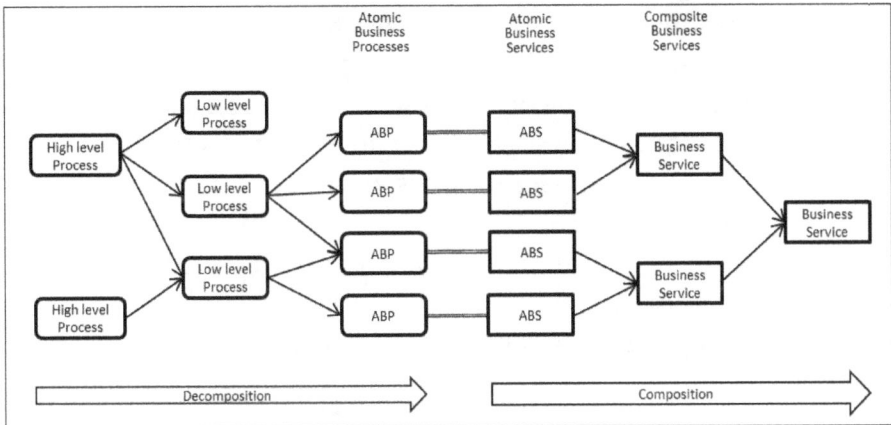

Figure 5a: Business Process decomposition

Once your atomic business processes have been identified and defined, you can start designing corresponding atomic business services. First, you translate the information flow requirements into message exchange patterns, then you translate the patterns and information flows into formal service contracts. This defines your most granular business services. Remember that you need to map not only data, but also behavior! All too often, these granular business services aren't used in isolation, often they are used within a workflow of services, so you may want to combine atomic business services into composite business services. These preferably - but not necessarily - map to corresponding composite business processes.

In a greenfield scenario way we often have the freedom to design services at will. Most of us will not have the luxury of a greenfield scenario: often we are constrained by existing legacy software. You might think the "Decomposition - Composition" approach illustrated in Fig. 5a will not work in a legacy environment: in fact it will work with minor adaptation, as illustrated in Fig 5b. You still decompose your business services to the atomic level, then design the corresponding atomic business services. Instead of building the services right away, you now first need to map the services to the legacy business applications. In this phase, you may run into mismatches between the designed service contracts and your legacy business applications. Basically, there are three ways to proceed:

- alter or add to your business applications (preferably, when possible)
- ignore or provide reconciliation logic (if it doesn't degrade the process)
- adjust the service contract (as a last resort)

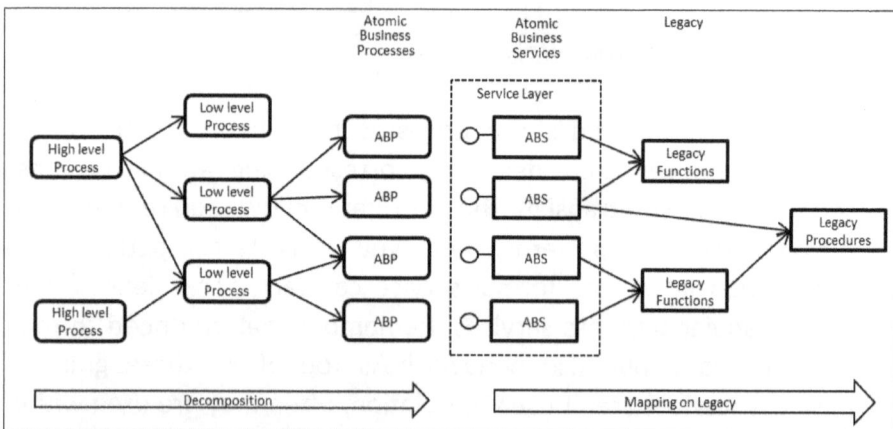

Figure 5b: Business Process decomposition in a legacy scenario

Before resorting to adjusting a service contract, remember that internal implementation details of a service should never be "leaked" to the outside. Once the mapping is done, you can start implementing the business services, thus creating a business service layer façade to your legacy applications.

Service Granularity

An often returning topic in discussions about integration services is how difficult it is to get the right service granularity. Is it really that difficult?

Granted, if you work bottom-up, trying to create services based on an existing datastore schema, or exposing existing functionality as services, finding the right service granularity is a hit-and-miss. Sadly, in practice we often start from IT systems already implemented, expose service interfaces from API's or data structures that already exist, and hope that business process requirements are met. Service contracts are not designed up-front, they are the haphazard result of the services that you expose.

However, working top-down, decomposing your business processes in various levels until you reach the level of atomic business processes (where further decomposition is senseless), the question of service granularity doesn't arise, that is, it has already been addressed in the decomposition phase. The level of atomic business processes represents the lowest granularity level of the services that you might wish to expose outside the boundaries of your system. The requirements of the business processes dictate the service contracts, thereby determining the service granularity.

Issues on service granularity only arise for finer-grained services, since these are not governed by corresponding business processes. Here trade-offs between reusability, genericity, flexibility, state, performance, legacy, context and more play a role in determining the granularity of a service. The interrelations between these aspects make the trade-off a very complex matter, but one of limited impact: since these finer-grained services should never be exposed outside the boundaries of the system to which they belong, thus limiting the impact of a trade-off, and potential reconsiderations, to only that system.

As far as software development is concerned, service granularity for business services is a given, determined by the business analyst or business architect through business process decomposition. For finer-grained services, service granularity is a trade-off of various aspects for the software developer to consider. This can be a difficult choice, since there is no fixed rule to follow, but the impact of a choice is limited and easily remedied.

Reuse of services is claimed to be one of the great benefits of this approach, so much so, that for many reuse has become a goal unto itself. It is not. Reuse is not a goal but a means to consolidate business logic and cut software development time and costs. This mode of working ensures that your services have the right granularity to optimally support your business processes, therefore reuse is the automatic byproduct.

Holistic Modeling, an oxymoron?

Whether or not a holistic model is an oxymoron depends on definitions. To most, it's pretty clear what modeling is, but I'll recap. Modeling is creating simplified representations of reality. A model has a purpose; the purpose dictates which aspects are relevant, and only relevant aspects need be present in the model. To obtain a better understanding, often several models of the subject are needed.

The term holistic is much less clear. To some, it means the comprehensive view on all parts of a system. When used in this sense, holistic modeling can indeed be regarded an oxymoron, since the basic concept of modeling is the omission of all parts deemed irrelevant for a certain purpose.

To most, the term holistic means focusing on the role that constituent parts play within a whole. As such, it would be the opposite of reductionism, the view that a system is but the sum of its parts, and that we can understand a system by analyzing its constituent parts.

Modeling how constituent parts work together should not be called holistic, but synthetic. Synthetic modeling on its own however, is not enough to get a deep grasp on the subject: we need both analytic and synthetic models. The combination of analytic modeling and synthetic modeling is what I would call holistic modeling. In this sense, holistic modeling is not an oxymoron, but a different approach to modeling.

Integration typically lies in the realm of holistic modeling. An integration interface is the implementation of the role that constituent part systems play to form a whole system (the word system being used here as a generic term for things like service, application, system, process etc.). One of the problems lies in the fact that today's tools and techniques are grafted on the reductionist, top-down approach, supporting analytic modeling. A tool or technique that supports synthetic modeling does not yet exist.

Another, even bigger, problem is that synthetic modeling involves non-linear, out-of-the-box thinking. IT people however, excel at reductionist

48

thinking, is which is linear. To our linear minds, synthetic thinking may seem chaotic and illogical. We fail to notice that reductionist thinking tends to create stovepiped solutions and often can lead to analysis paralysis.

For now, being aware that the traditional reductionist approach has significant limitations, is the first step towards holistic modeling. In the absence of a synthetic modeling tool or technique, some techniques in problem solving like Five Why's and Cause and Effect Analysis, and in general, abstracting away implementation details, may be very helpful in synthetic modeling.

5.5   Business process modeling

Many sometimes very divergent definitions have been given for a business process model. When mishmashing these definitions, we might conclude that a business process model is a multi-level description of the processes that an organization executes to fulfill its objectives, and the rules governing their execution, including the events that initiate those processes (triggers) and the results of those processes.

The multi-level qualification itself is two-dimensional: one dimension is that of scale: as illustrated in figure 5, a high level process can be divided into lower level processes, and this can be repeated until you reach a level of atomic business processes. The other dimension is the distinction between a logical business process model and an implementation business process model. Unfortunately this distinction is poorly supported in business process modeling tools, and in practice this distinction is not very often made.

The advantage of making this distinction is, that the logical model will be very stable; it will hardly, if ever, change. This allows for software to be divided into components along the same distinction: services that are built to the logical model, and clients that are built to the implementation model. The benefits of this approach are that your services inherit the stability of the logical model, and you can add, change and delete clients quickly and independently.

5.5.1   Business process requirements

As stated above, the sole purpose to buy or build enterprise application software is to support our business processes. It is the business process requirements that form the basis of the enterprise application software development or purchase lifecycle. As integrations holds the system of enterprise application software together, matching business process requirements is just as important for them.

Requirements gathering.

Every year since 1994 the Standish Group publishes their CHAOS report in which they focus on failures and possible improvements in IT projects. One of their findings is that requirements defects consistently ranks high in the top five causes for failed projects. In 2002 the share of costs attributable to requirements defects was estimated to be on average 56% of the total defect costs by the National Institute of Standards and Technology (NIST) in their "The Economic Impacts of Inadequate Infrastructure for Software Testing" report. Subsequent studies have not only shown the validity of this assessment, but have also shown no significant improvement over the years since the initial publications of the NIST and CHAOS reports.

One would think this should place a review of the requirements gathering process high on the agenda of every IT organization, but strangely, this is not the case. And yet there is a glaring gap that few seem to grasp. Three-tier (or multi-tier) architectures are common practice these days, so much so, that few if any organization continues to abide in monolithic architecture. To my mind, it is blatantly obvious that the requirements of a presentation layer are vastly different from the requirements of a business logic layer. One might even argue that user requirements are irrelevant for

---

a business logic layer. Still, most often the requirements gathering process takes the monolithic approach, eliciting requirements from users, customers and other stakeholders for an entire system, mingling user and business process requirements.

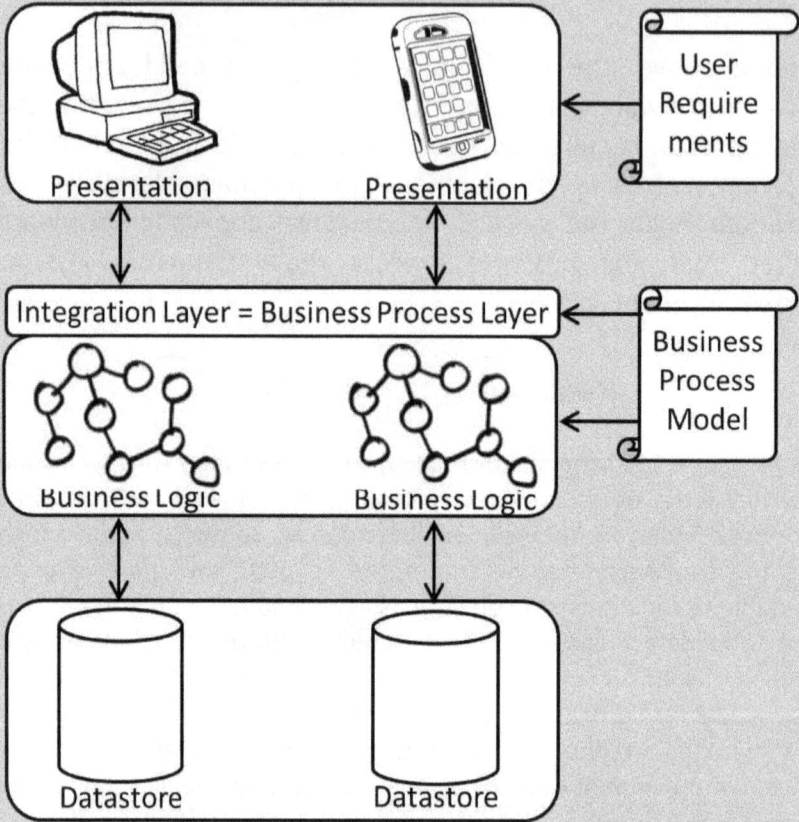

The first, indispensable step towards improvement of the requirements gathering process should be the explicit distinction between user requirements and business process requirements. The design of the presentation layer should be led by user requirements, the design of the business logic or services layer must be led by business process requirements. Traditional methods for requirements collection from users, customers and other stakeholders are still valid for eliciting user requirements regarding the presentation layer. The business process layer is better served with a different approach: start with a business process model, preferably detailed down to the level of atomic business processes, then have all human actors review the model. Once the model is validated, the business process requirements can be derived from the model.

This approach has a number of additional benefits: Solution proposals (as opposed to requirements) will be recognized as such more easily, and have less chance to contaminate your design. It allows you to think about your current and hopefully future business processes, addressing the adagio "Don't automate a process until you have optimized it." By separating the user interface it implicitly steers you in the direction of a more abstract model, thereby reducing interdependencies at the level where they hurt the most. Lastly, it invites and enables you to adopt business process management or BPM, a tool to keep your operations running optimally with the desired flexibility and speed.

Traditionally, business process requirements are defined at the start of an IT project. Unfortunately the focus and mindset of the participants in the project is geared toward the target software application, and often requirements with regard to data that is not owned by the process are overlooked. If then an adequate logical business process model is also lacking, all ingredients are there to produce a bad integration solution.

Business intelligence is an umbrella term that refers to gathering an organization's raw data for various activities like data mining, online analytical processing, querying and reporting. As such, it might be called a meta-business process; that is, it is a secondary business process that processes information about primary business processes. Since business intelligence gathers data from all primary business processes it is a large, if not the largest, client of integration services. It is essential to recognize that the requirements of the business intelligence processes govern these integration solutions, not the primary business process requirements. If a business intelligence solution uses a static snapshot of business process data, as is very often the case, then the requirements regarding integration are vastly different from requirements stemming from dynamic, active, real-time business processes (see also figure 2b). Technically, nothing precludes crossing over from one to the other. Normally, there is no problem to plug a business intelligence solution into an integration solution that is designed to primary business process requirements, but be very careful when plugging real-time business process applications into an integration solution that is designed to secondary business process requirements: it may well jeopardize the continuity of your primary business process support.

5.5.2 Information flow

An information flow is the communication of information between steps in the business processes. When these steps are supported within one software application, this information flow is often virtual and implicit. But when the steps are supported by two or more different software applications, the information flow must explicitly be implemented as a communication between these software applications.

For two (or more) partners to be able to communicate, the partners must agree on **how** to communicate. Just as in real life, when a sender sends messages over SMS, and the receiver expects to receive messages over email, no communication will take place. Not only do the communication partners need to agree on the technical protocol, they also need to agree on the language and the content. If the sender sends a message in Mandarin Chinese, and the receiver only understands Mexican Spanish, also no communication will take place. Neither will they communicate if the sender sends currency rates every week, and the receiver expects equity share values every five minutes.

The agreement on how to communicate should be consolidated into a communication contract. The communication contract describes everything that is needed to enable communication. It consists of a definition of the data that is conveyed, the address or addresses needed through which to communicate, the protocol to use, if and how to authenticate, and, finally, the communication pattern to use. The term communication contract is used loosely here: for W3C compliant soap/xml webservices the communication contract should be formally defined in a "wsdl" (web service definition language), for RESTful API's a "swagger" can formally define a communication contract; in other integrations, the communication contract may be informally descriptive.

5.6 The Vitruvius principles

As stated by Vitruvius, a good construction should satisfy the three principles of good architecture: *firmitas, utilitas et venustas*, (durability, functionality and elegance). For software solutions we have added a fourth principle: agility.

5.6.1 Durability

Ironically, while many constructions built by contemporaries of Vitruvius can be visited this day, not a single building attributed to Vitruvius himself has survived. The ability of constructions to survive two millennia depends on their reliability, robustness and resilience. The combination of these qualities is also known under the acronym R3. It is this aspect of durability, not longevity, that we seek in software architecture. Addressing R3 can build a system that can withstand, absorb, adapt, or recover from disturbances and disruptions.

We see a trend to address R3 lower and lower in the technology stack, so much so, that in many cases choosing the right transport protocol will suffice to address R3. You may think of redundancy, automatic failover and load balancing.

5.6.2 Functionality

Functionality is the ability of a system to do the work for which it was intended. A system's objective requires that many, most or all of the system's components work in a coordinated manner to complete the job, just as carpenters, electricians, plumbers, roofers and painters all need to cooperate to build a house. Therefore, if the components have not been assigned the correct responsibilities or do not have the correct facilities for coordination, the system will be unable to offer the required functionality. In civil architecture "Form Follows Function" is a principle associated with modern architecture and industrial design in the 20th century. The principle states that the shape of a building or object should be primarily based upon its intended function or purpose. The principle can also be applied to enterprise application solutions where "function" is the business processes which should be supported by architecture, or "form". "Form" does not dictate "function": it's the architect's task to arrange "form" to meet "function". "Function" may be achieved through any of a number of possible "forms". In fact, if functionality were the only requirement, any architecture would do. It is the combination of the four principles that determine in which situation which architecture is preferable over another.

5.6.3 Elegance

With "*venustas*" Vitruvius meant the 'truth of nature', his belief that nature's designs were based on universal laws of proportion and symmetry. His belief was almost spot on: nature's designs are based on universal laws which leads to proportion and symmetry.

The term elegance is hard to define; adjectives like graceful, tasteful, ingenious, seamlessly effortless and deceptively simple are often associated with elegance. Despite a lack of definition, most people will be able to recognize elegance when they encounter it. There are no rules to achieve elegance, but there are techniques that can help. One is decomposition, with which you can divide the problem space into components according to the blackbox principle, keeping the outside simple, and hiding the complexities inside. The other is abstraction, which is actually the same, but bottom-up. You use abstraction to hide the complex problem space as a blackbox behind a simple façade.

As with civil architecture, elegance cannot be achieved through tools or technology, following the handbook or dogged perseverance. It is the ingenuity and inspiration of the architect that provides the elegance of his solutions.

5.6.4   Agility

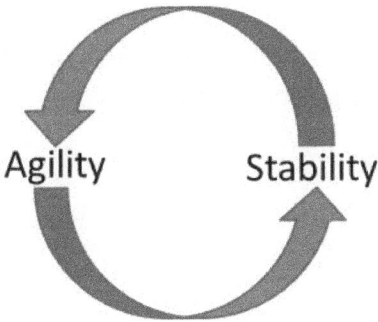

Fig 6 Agility & Stability

This is the fourth principle, and it was added because although the need for agility in civil architecture is virtually non-existent, in software architecture it is a very important, if not the most important driver. Agility is the ability of an organization to adapt or change quickly to succeed in a turbulent and ambiguous market.   James McGovern in his *"Practical Guide to Enterprise Architecture"* stated the need for agility in the following apparent paradox: *"Stability [. . .] is rooted in the ability to be dynamic, to move fast and change quickly"* while at the same time *"agility requires a stable foundation of things that don't change"*. While much of business agility depends on culture, a significant part lies in business process agility and the role of IT is an important factor in enabling this agility.

The same two techniques that can help to achieve elegance, decomposition and abstraction, will also help to achieve agility. Decomposition in particular will help in creating ready to use building blocks and abstraction, if done correctly, can provide the necessary stability. Applying other forms of loose-coupling patterns, like separation of execution and control and vertical layering, is another way to improve agility significantly. These measures allow for quick composition or even dynamic choreography of business services.

Note that the "Agile" software development methodology bears no direct relation to organizational agility: if anything, the area of tension between the "Agile" methodology and IT architecture may well lead to choices being made that hamper or impede agility.

It is interesting to note that of the four architecture principles only durability has any direct connection with tooling or technology.

6   The integration stack

Just as the OSI (Open System Interconnection) model provides a layered model, known as the OSI stack, as a conceptual framework to better understand communication protocols, so too we can provide a layered model called the integration stack, as a conceptual framework to better understand integration capabilities.

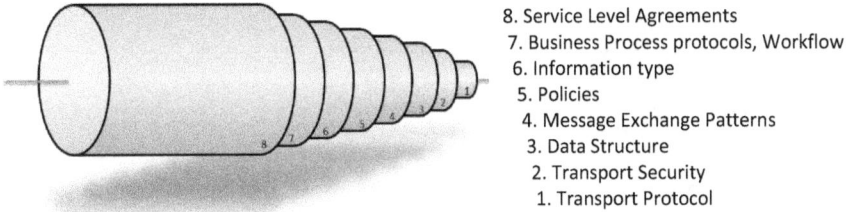

8. Service Level Agreements
7. Business Process protocols, Workflow
6. Information type
5. Policies
4. Message Exchange Patterns
3. Data Structure
2. Transport Security
1. Transport Protocol

Figure 7: Integration stack

There is not a real difference between the data integration stack and the application integration stack; there is merely a difference in emphasis on the various tiers, and a difference in the most common choices within each tier.

Realm	Tier		Examples	
Functio nality	Service Level Agreements	9	» 99.75% availability » 10.000 msgs/hour	
	Business Process Information Flow	8	» "PartsOrderReceived" » "StartSalaryRun"	A&A
	Information Type	7	» Event notification » Command	
	Policies	6	» Reliable Messaging » Signing	
Techno	Message Exchange Pattern	5	» Publish / Subscribe » Request / Response	

logy			
	4	Data Structure	» PDF » XML	
	3	Security	» Signing » Encryption	A&A
	2	Protocol	» Soap over HTTP » JMS	
	1	OS		

Table 2: Integration stack

As we have seen before, application integration is not merely sharing data between applications or systems, it is the implementation of information flows in business processes over the fabric of the applications network, to support these processes across heterogeneous and disparate applications and platforms. Therefore, when defining and designing integration solutions, the starting point is the definition of the business processes in general, and specifically the flow of information between them. Important aspects are the service level requirements that these business processes have and how the various policies that are applicable to the information flows are satisfied.

The information flows are always of a certain nature: for example, they might be an event notification or an information request; obviously, an event notification should be handled very differently from an information request. This information type is a decisive factor in establishing the message exchange pattern: if you signal an event, you typically don't care who will be receiving the event, and you don't wait for an answer of each of the receivers how they processed your event signal. On the other hand, when sending an information request, you normally know who to send the request to, and you typically expect a response.

Information is always structured: Only a random series of bits that are on or off is really unstructured. What is sometimes called unstructured information, is information whose structure isn't apparent at first sight, or whose structure is quite complicated. In straightforward information exchange, where content transformation, content enrichment or content based routing isn't applicable, structure may very well be irrelevant. When the content does become relevant, then so does the data structure. Some ways of structuring data are better suited for exchange than others.

In the end, it all boils down to communicating information between endpoints, and there is a huge variety in protocols to realize that communication. Theoretically, you can implement any message exchange pattern with any protocol, in practice, some combinations are perfect, some are acceptable, and some are downright impractical.

6.1 Authentication & Authorization

Literally, authentication (from Greek: αὐθεντικός "real, genuine") is the act of confirming the truth of a piece of data. In the IT world, the meaning of authentication is often narrowed down to verifying the identity of a subject. Authorization defines whether an authenticated subject can perform an action on a particular object. Identity management addresses the multi-faceted problem of how subjects are given identities and how these identities are propagated. Access Management on the other hand aims to grant authorized users the right to use a service, while preventing access to non-authorized users.

The integration stack has two levels where authentication and authorization partake: the first level is on the transport protocol level, the second is on the business process level. A second aspect is the authentication protocol for propagating an identity to the higher levels of the stack; this can take place at the transport security level, or at the policies level.

6.1.1 Protocol level Authentication & Authorization

Protocol level authentication and authorization involves granting or denying permission for a specific service to use a specific protocol. Protocol level authentication and authorization should not be defined for end-users; rather it should be defined for services that are subject to authentication and authorization on the business process level.

6.1.2 Business process level Authentication & Authorization

Business process level authentication and authorization involves granting or denying access for a business resource[1] to use a specific business resource[2], where business resource[1] is most often an end-user, but may also be a business object, service or function, and business resource[2] is typically a business service, but may also be a business object or function. The decision to grant or deny access to a specific resource is commonly based on one, or a combination of, the following four access controls:

- Consumer-based access control: Manage access to an object based on the consumer of a service. For example, ensure that only the Order Service may invoke operation "getCreditLimit(accountId)" on the BusinessPartner Service.
- RBAC: Role-based access control: Manage access to an object based on the role or roles that a subject is affiliated with. For example, the ability to remove a business partner could be granted to any user with an "Account Admin" role.
- ABAC: Attribute-based access control: Manage access to an object based on inherent attributes of the subject or object. For example, only Account Admins from the UK market (subject attribute) may alter data on customers from Great Britain (object attribute).
- Time-based access control: Manage access to an object based on the time of day or calendar date - for instance, "only allow changes to accounts during normal business hours, Mon – Fri, 08:00 – 17:00 hrs".

6.1.3 Claims based access control

Claims based access control is a powerful abstraction of identity and access management. It can minimize the need to implement identity and access capabilities in applications, and enables a single sign-on to access various applications. Another benefit of claims based access is that on one side it allows user anonymity, on the other side it can provide extended attributes associated with the user.

A claim is a statement about a subject, the claim can be an identity, a role or any attribute that you can assign to a subject. Claims are not what the subject can and cannot do. They are what the subject is or is not. It is up to the application receiving the incoming claim to map the 'is / is not' claims to the 'may / may not' rules of the application. Claims based access control allows the burden of authenticating what a subject is or is not (the claims) to be shifted from your solutions to an identity provider outside your solution. The claims do not specify what authorizations a subject has or does not have: it is up to the application receiving the claim to determine the authorizations based on what the claim declares a subject is or is not. You can use claims to implement role-based access control (RBAC), attribute-based access control (ABAC) or a combination of the two. Roles are claims, and claims can contain attributes too. Claims based access control is further discussed in the Policies paragraph.

6.2 Transport Protocol

Within the context of this book, Transport Protocol refers to the topmost layer of the OSI Reference Model for network data traffic, the Application Layer or Layer 7. Notice that the OSI Model is an excellent example of reducing complexity by introducing levels of indirection.

There is a huge variety of data transport protocols, and in principle, any of them can be used in application integration, though some are more suitable than others. Some of the most popular ones include HTTP, FTP, SMTP, NFS, Telnet, SNMP, POP3, NNTP and IRC. Some protocols provide support for implicit or explicit security: authorization to use the protocol is covered in the previous paragraph, propagating security information to the higher levels will be covered in the next paragraph. Transport Protocol constitutes the first layer over the operating system. Loose-coupling starts at the protocol level: to ensure interoperability, avoid OS dependent protocols, or provide protocol adapters.

6.3   Transport Security

The transport security that safeguards the communication channel between applications has two main components:
- the security of the information flowing through the channel.
- the propagation of authentication through the channel.

Both are briefly explained below.

6.3.1   Information security.

Information security is aimed at preventing unauthorized access, use, disclosure or manipulation of information. Information security at the transport level has two main aspects:
- Confidentiality (the data transported is cannot be intercepted, or cannot be read when intercepted).
- Message integrity (the data is checked for possible corruption).

The information flowing through a communication channel can be secured by either preventing interception by unauthorized parties, or by encrypting the information, so the intercepted stream cannot be read by unauthorized parties. Implicitly, transport layer encryption precludes intentional content manipulation, thus addressing both confidentiality and integrity concerns. Transport protocols that are not implicitly secure require additional measures to ensure that security requirements are met. With secure transport protocols, the following must be kept in mind:
- Consider transport security for each step between nodes, but be aware that the nodes themselves may not be secure.
- Transport level security means that information is protected only while in transit on the wire; the stores where the information is kept before it is sent and after it is received need explicit protection.

- Element signing or encryption is not supported; instead the entire datastream will be encrypted.
- Integrity is not guaranteed, meaning data can be compromised, but compromised data will be recognized as such.
- Non-repudiation is not supported.

Some of the most commonly used transport protocols for integration solutions are listed in table 3. In the column "Secure" the following symbols are used:

☺ = acceptable level of encryption to ensure confidentiality

☹ = no or insufficient level of encryption to ensure confidentiality

☺ = further addressed in column "Remarks"

Data Transport	Secure	Remarks
read/write	☺	
read/write over LAN	☺	
read/write over WAN	☺	Fairly secure when using a VPN
HTTP	☹	Plain transport over TCP/IP
HTTPS	☺	Encrypted transport over TCP/IP
FTP	☹	Plain transport over TCP/IP
FTPS	☺	Encrypted transport over TCP/IP
SFTP	☺	Encrypted transport over TCP/IP, enhanced authentication support
WCF Custom JavaBeans	☺	In principle, various standards of signing, hashing and encrypting can be used. However, much depends on the capabilities of the associated endpoint.
SCP	☺	Encrypted transport over TCP/IP, enhanced authentication support

MSMQ	🙂	Microsoft proprietary when native (not over HTTP 🙁)
Websphere MQ	🙂	IBM proprietary
iDoc, RFC	🙂	SAP proprietary
AMQP	🙂	Uses SASL
MQTT	🙂	V3.1 and higher supports SSL encryption and credentials authentication at a significant performance cost
SMTP	🙁	Plain content over TCP/IP
SMTPS	🙂	Encrypted transport over TCP/IP
POP3	🙁 🙂	Plain content over TCP/IP, may use encrypted transport
IMAP	🙁 🙂	Plain content over TCP/IP, may use encrypted transport
ODBC	🙁 🙂	Plain content over TCP/IP, may use encrypted transport

Table 3: Transport level security

Remember that this table only provides a global overview of security at the transport protocol level; it does not mean that protocols that do not address security implicitly cannot be used for transport of security sensitive information. It means that for security sensitive information additional measures must be taken to secure the transport over these protocols.

6.3.2 Authentication protocols.

The main responsibility of an authentication protocol is enabling a server/service to verify a connecting party's identity. Some protocols also support authenticating server/service to the connecting party. In the early years we only had the PAP protocol. Due to its vulnerabilities, many different authentication protocols have since been defined. For integration, the following list of authentication protocols is relevant:

- PAP (Password Authentication Protocol): this involves sending credentials (username and password). When used for setting up a connection (like HTTP or FTP) it is highly insecure since the credentials are transmitted in plain ASCII text. Because of its simplicity, it still is widely used, and most transport protocols will support this authentication protocol.
- CHAP (Challenge-Handshake Authentication Protocol): Server sends a random challenge Client uses this challenge and his password to calculate a MD5 hash over his username and sends the hash together with his username in plain text. Server performs the same calculation and compares the calculated and received hash. It's a safe protocol, but used primarily by PPP servers.
- EAP Extensible Authentication Protocol is a part of the IEEE 802.1x authentication framework. It provides common functions and negotiation of authentication methods. The most commonly implemented EAP method is TLS, better known as SSL. SSL uses a combination of secret-key and public-key cryptography to secure communications: secret keys for encryption and decryption, and public keys for authentication. For websites, SSL is most often used in one-way mode, where the server authenticates itself by sending the client a certificate. A typically example is online banking. For integration scenario's, the two-way mode where both client and server authenticate themselves to each other by sending certificates to each other is more commonly used.
- NTLM (NT LAN Manager) is a suite of Microsoft security protocols that provides authentication, integrity and confidentiality on the OS level within a Microsoft network.
- Kerberos uses symmetric key cryptography and requires a trusted third party to provide mutual authentication over an open network within a domain, or over trusted domains. Kerberos dwells on top of the OS level.

It is beyond our scope to go further into the technical details of transport protocols and transport security. It is however important to note that choices on other levels of the integration stack influence the suitability of the transport protocols.

6.4 Data Structure or technical information content

Obviously, the provider in an integration service will send data in a certain structure or format, and just as obviously, the client of an integration service must know the structure or format of the data it receives, if it wants to process that information. Without one or more *controllers* between provider and client, this is a form of tight-coupling: if any provider or client needs a change in the structure or format, all providers and clients will need to change simultaneously.

Versioning, having two or more recognizable versions of a structure, is one way to mitigate this problem. When a receiver of a message supports two or more versions of message structure, it is up to the sender, which version will be sent. Thus the sender can change version independently from the receiver. Some structures have built-in versioning.

The other way of mitigation is, as we saw before, the introduction of a *controller* or a *mediator*. A controller may come in the form of a standard that determines the structure or format of the data. A mediator could be a broker or bus or anything that can transform the structure or format of the information.

There is a myriad of ways to structure and format data, but broadly, we can categorize them as follows:

Message Content		examples	Data element format	Versioning support
Unstructured	Positional text		No	No
	Comma separated		No	No
Structured	Text based	EDI, SWIFT	Yes	Yes
	Binary	mdb, pdf, excel	Yes	No
	XML	self-describing, schema	Yes	Yes
	Json	self-describing, schema	Yes	No
	Domain model	ebXml, SEPA	Yes	Yes

Table 4: Message content types

Information that is shared between endpoints needs to be structured in a way that these endpoints recognize and support. Of course the so-called "unstructured" message content is also structured, but in a way that is not immediately recognizable or self-evident.

- Positional text; this structure relies on a sequence of *records*. These *records* can be of one or more *recordtypes*. Each data element has a fixed position and a fixed length within a certain *recordtype*. Because of this, this type of structure is also known as "Fixed Format". In the early years we saw a lot of these. There is no shared understanding of the representation of non-text data-elements like dates, times, or decimals.
- CSV; this structure also relies on a sequence of records. Usually, these records have the same structure, but records of several recordtypes are possible. Each data element appears in a fixed order within a certain recordtype. The data elements are separated from each other by a separator

character. The name "Comma Separated Values" suggests to use a comma as separator character, but in fact any character will do. Special attention must be given to data elements that may contain the separator character. As for positional files, there is no shared understanding of the representation of non-text data-elements.

- Under "text based" (the name is chosen due to lack of a better name) the structures are grouped that are based on positional or separated text, but are further defined by standardization organizations for a specific functional domain; good examples are EDI for the logistics domain, and SWIFT for monetary transactions. For the most part, these are legacy standards, and many of these standards are moving away from text-based towards xml-based schema's.

- Binary: Under "technical proprietary" we typically group known file formats that have become de facto standards, examples are Excel files, MS Access databases or Adobe PDF files. Whereas exchange of these kind of files between natural persons is very common, using these filetypes for application integration is questionable.

- XML, eXtensible Markup Language, is a structure for encoding documents in a generic format that is both human-readable and machine-readable, governed by the W3C standards. It can be loose-types, or strong typed by using XML schema's. W3C's design goal for XML was generality and usability across all platforms. As such, it is ideally suited for the exchange of information in general, but also ideally suited as a base for domain standards.

- JSON, JavaScript Object Notation, is a format that uses human-readable text to transmit data objects consisting of attribute–value pairs. The format is not formally defined, but the json.org organization is emerging as a *de facto* authority. In much the same sense, there is no formal json description convention, but the swagger.io organization is emerging as a *de facto* authority, promoting "swagger" schema's to strong type json messages. Generic conversion between JSON and XML vice-versa is possible, provided the json.org standard is followed.

6.5   Message Exchange Pattern or MEP

The most important characteristic of an interface is which communication pattern to use, formally known as Message Exchange Pattern or MEP. Table 5 illustrates the most important basic MEP's. More message exchange patterns have been described, but they are either unsuitable for integration purposes, or an extension or combination of the basic MEP's mentioned as follows.

	MEP		Receivers	Push Pull	Real-life example	Sync / Async
FF	Fire & Forget a.k.a. datagram	send an event signal	undefined	Push	SOS alarm	async
RR	Request / Response	send a request and wait for one response	1	Pull	Push traffic light button	sync
SR	Solicit / Response a.k.a. Request / Callback	send a request and (at some time) receive one (or more) response(s)	1	Pull		async
PS	Publish / Subscribe a.k.a. Observer	send an event signal to none, one or more receivers	0..n	Push	News broadcast	async
HD	Half-Duplex	arbitrary number of messages to be sent by a client and received in turn	1	any	Walkie-Talkie conversation	sync

| FD | Full-Duplex | arbitrary number of messages to be sent by a client and received in any order simultaneously | 1 | any | Telephone conversation | sync |

Table 5: Basic message exchange patterns

In layman's terms you might call a message exchange pattern a 'communication service type'. If you look at the column 'Real-Life example' in table 5, you'll notice familiar but very different forms of communication. You might call them communication services of a particular type: e.g. a newspaper is a communication service of the publish / subscribe type.

Another important characteristic of an information flow is the size of the information being exchanged. Large messages should be treated differently than smaller messages. A practical limit says that smaller messages are normally smaller than 100 Kb, and never exceed 4 Mb in size; large messages are often larger than 100 Kb, or can possibly exceed 4 Mb in size. Whereas theoretically the same MEP's apply for small and large messages, in practice only the asynchronous MEP's are technically feasible for large data volumes, and of these only the Fire-and-Forget MEP is particularly relevant.

Three base message exchange patterns are essential and should be addressed in detail: these exchange patterns are Request/Response and Fire & Forget for small messages, and Fire & Forget for large messages, better known as Managed File Transfer. Half-Duplex and Full-Duplex are also base message exchange patterns, but since their relevance in application integration and data integration is questionable, these patterns probably do not need to be addressed. There are many more elaborate message exchange patterns, but these are derivations, specializations or composites of the three base message exchange patterns mentioned above. To illustrate, you can think of a "Submit" message exchange pattern, consisting of an initial synchronous RR, asynchronously followed by one or more FF messages.

ACME offers a "SubmitOrder" webservice, where its dealers can submit a json or XML formatted "SubmitOrderRequest" message. Upon receiving a valid request message, the service immediately returns an empty HTTP 200 response to acknowledge the receipt of the request message. At the same time, it forwards the message to the legacy system that does the order processing. The legacy ordering process will generate progress notifications. If the dealer has specified a queuing mechanism, these progress notifications will be sent to it, otherwise, ACME also offers a webservice that allows dealers to track the progress of their order.

6.6 Policies

Within the context of this book, a policy is a principle of action, applied to a service, adopted by the architecture board and enforced through governance. Policies have a scope (i.e. global, local, business service, message type), and the prescribed principle of action can vary from very generic to very specific.

You may publish the policies that apply to a service with WS-Policy, an XML specification for services to advertise their policies and for service consumers to specify their policy requirements. In principle any policy can be published through WS-Policy, but for some topics various standards have been proposed, some of which are widely adopted:
- WS-SecurityPolicy
- WS-RM (Reliable Messaging)
- WS-AtomicTransaction
- WS-Federation

While these WS policies are specified to be used for SOAP/XML webservices, most of the specifications can be used for any other form of digital communication. Some policies you might think of applying are:

- Reliable Message Delivery
  Message delivery reliability ensures a guarantee that either a message is delivered, or you receive feedback that the message could not be delivered. This guarantee can be implemented on various layers in the integration stack: the transport protocol, the message exchange pattern and even the business process flow. Using durable messages and durable subscriptions through message queueing is the default way to implement reliable message delivery on the transport level. Various message queueing solutions are available, among which are MSMQ, AMQP, JMS and

73

WebSphere MQ. The policy sets the reliability requirements. Whether these reliability requirements can be met will depend how the message queueing solution is configured, and how it is addressed. Be aware that synchronous communication precludes a 100% reliable message delivery: synchronous communication implies a potential time-out, and there is no way to establish whether the time-out occurred on the request or on the response message.

- Error handling
  It is essential to differentiate between technical errors and functional errors, since they will be handled differently. Technical errors have to be addressed by technical application managers. Examples of technical errors are:
  - The service cannot be reached
  - An unexpected exception has occurred
  - A software client is not allowed to use a specific service

Functional errors have to be addressed by functional application managers or end-users. Examples of functional errors are:
  - Unknown vehicle ID
  - Value out of range
  - An end-user is not allowed to use a specific service

The policy prescribes generically or in detail how to log and handle all or each of the potential errors. Error handling may depend on message exchange pattern and information type. For example, the broadcaster of event notifications is not interested in receiving feedback on the reception or processing of the event notifications it publishes.

- Retry
  You might specify a Retry policy for failing communications. The applicability of this policy may depend on failing reason or message exchange pattern. When the communication fails because of a functional error, it probably will make no sense to retry, since each retry will fail again. For some technical errors (i.e. "server too busy", "database deadlock") a retry policy is useful, since the error cause may very well be resolved by the time it is retried. Use caution when specifying a retry policy for synchronous communication: in case of a time-out it is not clear whether the time-out occurred before or after the request was processed. In this case, specify a retry policy only when the addressed service is idempotent, or in plain words, can handle duplicate messages.

- Frequency
  To prevent Denial-of-Service attacks, or just service overloading, a frequency policy may be specified. Web services are especially vulnerable to overloading, so it makes sense to a frequency policy. Solutions based on message queueing are much more resistant to overloading, but even here, since messages must be temporarily stored, you may consider the data volume, the ingoing and outgoing speed, and the potential choke and throttling, to decide if a frequency policy should be specified.

- Atomic Transaction
  A transaction policy specifies how to ensure that when invoking a set of services, either all succeed, or none succeeds. Implementing a transaction scope over services will at best be very cumbersome, and chances are that you will introduce more issues than you hope to cure.

More often than not, the use of WS-AtomicTransaction is the result of bad service design or bad architectural decisions. Services should be loosely coupled and autonomous, thus precluding the need for a transaction scope. Indeed, the premise of this book, to base your integration services on your business processes, eliminates the need for a transaction policy, at least on the level of business services. At lower levels the need might still arise, but a reengineering of the software is probably to be preferred over using a transaction scope over service invocations.

- Security Policies
Securities three main areas of interest are authentication (the assurance of a party's identity), confidentiality (the assurance that unauthorized parties cannot access certain information) and integrity (the assurance that information has not been altered). The WS-Security policy addresses all three; it specifies the use of security tokens to ensure authentication, it specifies encryption methods to assure confidentiality and it specifies signing methods to assure integrity; the latter also addresses non-repudiation (the assurance that a party cannot deny having performed a certain action).
The WS-Security specification allows a variety of signature formats, encryption algorithms and multiple trust domains, and is open to various security token models. Amongst others, X.509 certificates, Kerberos tickets, username / password credentials and SAML assertions are supported. As stated earlier, the WS-Security specifications can easily be implemented for other forms of digital communication.
Authentication and confidentiality, and (up to a certain level) integrity can also be addressed at other levels of the integration stack, see the paragraphs on Authentication &

Authorization and Transport Security. Combinations and trade-offs are possible.

- Audit
  Whereas the security policy addresses security upfront, an audit policy addresses security afterwards. An audit policy allows to track potential security problems, helps to ensure user accountability, and may provide evidence in the event of a security breach. The policy specifies the events that need to be logged, and the information that needs to be logged with them.

6.7 Information Type or functional information content

The sixth layer of the integration stack concerns the functional information content, or the nature of the information. The categories that we distinguish are:

Info Type	Description
Objects	With an object a representation of an instance of a business entity is meant; it is specifically not an instance of a class in an object-oriented programming language. The representation or model of a business entity is a logically coherent set of structured or unstructured attributes (that itself may or may not be entities) that may be mutable or immutable. When used in an interface, they are static snapshots of business objects, which by themselves are not suitable for supporting dynamic (near) real-time integration. As a component of another message they can be very useful: for example, a PartsOrderReceived message might consist of two items: a datetime of reception, and an entire PartsOrder object.

Commands	Commands are instructions to a system to execute some unit of work. With "unit of work" is meant the (set of) logic that supports a business process, independent of its level. It is a bad practice to let business applications implement a workflow by generating and sending commands, since that obscures the workflow in the application code, impedes agility, and tightly couples applications. Better let an orchestration application, such as a workflow engine, a business rule engine, or the ESB itself, issue the commands. Having a workflow engine or ESB receiving event messages, and creating command-type messages based on these received event messages makes the system of solutions much more agile and robust, and enables much better visibility and control. This principle is known as "Separation of control and execution", and this is a sound architectural principal to enable agility in business processes. Conversely, in situations where a new higher-level business process is started, often triggered by a human decision, it is advisable to let a business application generate and send a command-type message.
Events	Event messages are notifications of events that have taken place. Often one or more business objects are involved with these events. The event message will contain the key identifiers to these business object(s), and the set of attributes that is relevant to the event. Typically, event messages are broadcasted to all systems that are allowed and interested to receive these messages. It is up to these "clients" if and/or how they handle, interpret and follow up on these event messages. Whether a client can handle, interpret and follow up on an event message is of no concern to the originator: the event message is the broadcast of an event that has taken place, irrespective of any client handling such message.

N.B. It is critical to understand that we are referring to business events, not "CRUD" events in a data store. |

Request messages	A distinction is made between services that retrieve information, and services that process information. The retrieval services are addressed with "request" messages. Usually, a request message can be quite small, or even be absent. Often, it contains only some identifying attributes. For example, to retrieve the current time using a GetCurrentTime() service, you would not need to use a request message, though you might think of a GetCurrentTimeRequest message that contains a location element, to retrieve the current time at the desired location. Usually, request messages are handled synchronously, and as such have a corresponding response message. Process messages on the other hand are usually larger, since they contain information that needs to be processed. For example, the ValidateOrderRequest will at least contain an entire Order. Process messages can be handled synchronously or asynchronously: various aspects determine which communication pattern will be most suitable. Request messages that involve an obviously asynchronous business process are regarded as a special subtype: submit messages.
Submit messages	Submit messages are a special type of request message. As stated for the previous bullet, a distinction is made between services that retrieve information, and services that process information. Often, a submit message contains an entire object, or a cohesive set of objects. Normally, submit messages are handled asynchronously, but they may be received by a synchronous endpoint. In that case, the synchronous response needs to be no more than an acknowledgement of reception.
Acknowledgements	Acknowledgements are short or even empty messages that acknowledge the receipt of a request or submit message. In case of an empty message it is the metadata associated with it (e.g. HTTP Response code 200) that provide the acknowledgement. In case of an non-empty message, the contents could be a copy of the received message, or an ID under which the received message was registered.

Response messages	Response messages are messages that are returned to the sender of a request message after reception and possibly processing, usually synchronously. Obviously, the content of the response message depends on the request, but the cohesion requirement prohibits an haphazard set of attributes and demands an object or at the very least a coherent set of attributes.
Models	Models are a special type of response or object message. Instead of the (partial) representation of one object, this object message contains a coherent set of objects and the relation(s) between them. For example, you may think of a generic service that returns a composite list of countries, with per country the set of supported languages, the set of supported currencies with their daily exchange rate, and the set of VAT tariffs. A client might address this service once to load the entire structure in memory. Use with care.
"Records"	This refers to the contents of database tables or other data sources. It is the classical way of legacy applications to exchange data. In modern applications this should be avoided, since it can, and often will, introduce all kinds of technical problems with respect to platform dependency, sorting, batching, referential integrity, transaction scope and more. It also creates dependencies between the partners of an interface: they must be aware of their respective implementation details. The exchange of "records" should never be considered for support of operational services. Only in specific cases like data replication for off-loading or non-operational database downloads for analysis purposes, the gathering and transport of "records" may be considered.

| Composite records | This refers to the practice of combining various data elements into one set, to be exchanged with another system. This kind of messages are almost always driven by the information need of one particular client, and not at all triggered by business events or driven by business information flows. Composite records, as opposed to business objects, tend to violate the coherence principle: if a set of data elements is coherent, then it is probably a good (subset of a) representation of a business object. Using composite records is therefore rarely advisable; it generally is bad in pull scenarios because of coherence issues, and even worse in push scenarios because the lack of a business trigger leads to timing issues and unnecessary traffic. Consider exchanging business events instead. |

Table 6: Information Types

Technically you can send any information type in any situation using any message exchange pattern; in practice, some combinations make sense while other combinations are pointless. Table 7 lists the most common combinations of when to use which information type.

Information Type	When to use
Events	From processes, use business events, not CRUD triggers
Commands	From orchestration, choreography or workflow
Request messages	Request to receive information
Submit messages	Request to execute an action
Acknowledgements	Receipt acknowledgement to a submit message
Response messages	Response to a request or submit message
Objects	Data Integration
Models	Replication
Records	Data Integration
Composite records	Don't use

Table 7: When to use the information types

Objects in object-oriented programming languages, while perfectly suited for communication within a solution, should never be exchanged outside their solution, to avoid unwanted dependencies and communication problems.

6.8 Business Process protocols and Workflow

Business processes are conventionally modeled as monolithic flows that capture the desired business logic in terms of the flow of its execution. These monolithic flows are often needlessly complicated or complex and restrict the autonomy of its participants, limiting agility. Modularizing or decomposing monolithic business processes as illustrated in figure 5 allows for clear separation of concerns for both modeling and executing the processes, thus improving agility and . Modularization or decomposition into fine grained or atomic business services introduces the need to choreograph or orchestrate them to cooperate. This choreography can be done in code, resulting in monolithic services which we tried to avoid in the first place by decomposing. The other way to implement this choreography is through business process protocols or workflows, which enables configurable, sometimes even dynamic, definition of said choreography.

Many workflow management and workflow automation solutions are available, most of which use a proprietary language to design and execute their workflows. In addition, most message broker and message bus solutions also provide process design and execution support.

Several standards have been proposed for the specification and/or execution of business process protocols, the best known are:
- BPEL (Business Process Execution Language), is an XML-based standard executable language proposed by OASIS for specifying actions within business processes. BPEL aims to model the behavior for both Executable and Abstract Business Processes.
- BPMN (Business Process Model and Notation), is a graphical representation for specifying business processes in a business process model, similar to activity diagrams in UML.

The primary goal of BPMN is to provide a standard notation method which is readily understandable by business stakeholders. It includes an informal and partial mapping from BPMN to BPEL enabling BPMN models to be exported as executable BPEL.

- ebXML is a family of XML based standards proposed by OASIS to standardize the secure exchange of business data. As such, it cannot be used as a choreography tool; it is comparable to EDI, and more suited to standardize business process interaction.
- XLANG/s is a Microsoft language similar (but not portable) to C#. It is primarily used in MS BizTalk, where it is generated through an Orchestration Designer GUI. After compilation it is able to execute the orchestrations.

Basically, there are two ways to design a choreography:
- Sequential: A sequential workflow represents the most basic set of control structures: sequence, iteration and selection. It models a set of preconceived paths from a start state to a final state. Sequential workflows are therefore quite rigid. Sequential workflow models tend to grow exponentially in size and complexity with added inputs. This type of modeling may be considered for controlling simple business processes.
- State Machine: A state machine workflow represents a set of states, transitions, and actions. The steps in a state machine workflow execute asynchronously. This means that they are not necessarily performed one after another, but instead are triggered by actions and states. One state is assigned as the start state, and then, based on an event, a transition is triggered to another state. The state machine can have a final state that determines the end of the workflow. A state machine model is much more apt at modeling behavior than a sequential model. This type of modeling may be

considered for supporting any business process, and is the best choice for all but the most simple processes.

Although a simple sequential workflow is much easier to design than a simple state machine, a state machine is much easier to alter or adjust than a sequential workflow. It is therefore recommended to always design as a state machine, unless changes afterwards are unlikely. In the end, there is no point in achieving agility by decomposition and choreography, only to lose agility by defining sequential workflows. The focus of the state machine models on events that trigger actions make them the ideal way to model the choreography of messages and services.

6.9 Service Level Requirement/Agreement

It is a pertinacious misconception that Service Level Requirements (SLR's) and Service Level Agreements (SLA's) must be defined for software solutions. It is not the software solution that has service level requirements, it is the business process that has service level requirements, and it is up to the software solutions that are needed in that business process to fulfill these requirements. The problem with application based SLA's becomes painfully clear when considering integration solutions: even the simplest integration, where a business process is supported by two software applications, can have three very different service level agreements if we forget to look at business process requirements.

A service level agreement or SLA formally defines the availability, reliability, performance and quality of delivered services to ensure the right information is passed safely and securely between the right endpoints at the right time. Traditionally, the SLA is specified per software application between service provider and service client, but with the notion that integration forms the bonding in a system of systems, this approach has become far too simple.

Since an integration service is but one component in a system of systems that supports the business processes, it is the service level requirements of the business process(es) that dictates the service level requirements of the components in a system of systems. Here too, the age old adage about the weakest link applies; it is therefore important to establish in which business processes the service plays a role before a service level agreement can be specified.

Specifying a very high service level requirement will have consequences for the design of a solution. You might think of having two or more implementations of the same service with different SLA's; for example a slow service with a high SLA, and a fast service with a lower SLA.

7 Synthesis

As we have seen earlier, the distinction between data integration and application integration is vital. The fabric of the application network consists of the application integration layer that exposes the business logic captured in Line-of-Business applications. It does so to allow operational workers (whether human or non-human) to manage the execution of business process instances. Generally it is bidirectional and real-time in nature. The data integration layer on the other hand provides the data to manage a business process as a whole, to be presented to business process managers. Generally it is unidirectional in nature, and covers historical data. What emerges is a picture of two stacks, the applications stack and the business intelligence stack.

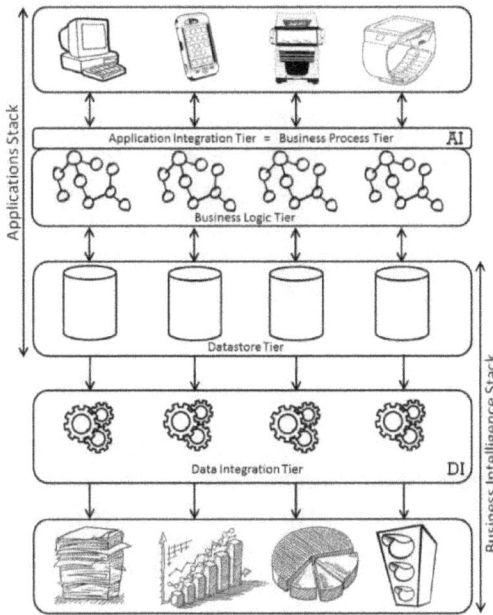

Figure 8: Integration in a multi-tier architecture

The two stacks have a shared datastore tier, but each has its own integration tier. The capabilities that we require from these two integration tiers are the same, but as shown above, the nature of the information that flows through these tiers on the whole is entirely different.

A good practice is to consolidate all integration capabilities in one place, an integration hub, suite, bus or even just a collection of integration tools. A good question then is whether you want one integration hub to support both the application and data integration tier, or you want each of the integrations tier to have its own integration hub. Both options have its pros and cons.

	One single Integration hub	Two or more Integration hubs
Architecture	Needs a generic architecture to allow both DI and AI.	Allows specific architectures for each hub; e.g. broker architecture for the DI hub and ESB architecture for the AI hub.
Tooling	Single set of tooling, consolidated capabilities.	Some to all of the tooling will have to be deployed twice.
Message Exchange Patterns	Less control over when and how to use, and how to implement the various message exchange patterns.	Better control over when and how to use, and how to implement; this may very well be different for DI and AI.
Design-Time Governance	No separate policies for DI and AI solutions possible. One hub for all clients. DI and AI solutions are lumped together. Consolidated configuration.	Integrations must explicitly be deployed in DI or AI. Clients must know which hub to address. Separate policies can be applied to DI and AI hubs and solutions. Distributed configuration.
Run-Time Governance	Consolidated management and monitoring. A single set of Service Level Requirements/Agreements applies.	Distributed management and monitoring. You can specify separate sets of Service Level Requirements/Agreements.
Operational	AI and DI solutions will be competing for resources. DI solutions tend to be voluminous and may severely hinder AI solutions.	Aside from some endpoints, AI and DI use independent resources.

Ownership / Responsibility	Different ownership for DI and AI solutions on a single hub may prove awkward.	Easily allows different ownership for DI and AI hubs and solutions. DI might be positioned as an integral part of Business Intelligence.

Table 8: Single vs Dual hub

Using data integration techniques in the business process environment, in situations where application integration is called for, guarantees an ill-fitting support threatening the continuity of the actual business processes. Only when certain conditions are met can data integration techniques sometimes be used in a business process environment, for example for local copies of master data that rarely change, or only change at set intervals such as daily exchange rates. The reverse is less problematic, application integration techniques may be used in a business intelligence environment, though most often this will not be the best choice.

Although several commonalities exist between the two, the difference in their patterns is essential. The commonalities can be seen as capabilities that can be shared between data and application integration. The difference in patterns warrants a separate approach.

7.1 Data Integration

To a lot of people, the term data integration architecture sounds like an oxymoron, because they don't think that data integration has its own architecture. Many data warehouse professionals still cling to practices of the 1990's, when data integration was part of the larger data warehouse architecture. Today, many data integration specialists continue to design and build one independent ETL process after the other, a poor practice that's inherently anti-architectural. A common misconception is that using a vendor product for data integration automatically assures architecture.

Data integration concerns the flow of data from diverse source systems (typically operational applications for ERP, CRM, supply chain management etc. where most enterprise data originates) through often multiple transformations to be presented in diverse target systems (typically non- operational applications like data warehouses, customer data hubs, and product catalogs). For both data sources and targets heterogeneity in data storage, platform and protocol is the norm. Also, different data models require data to be transformed, and the transforms themselves vary widely. The endpoint of the interfaces that connect these pieces are equally diverse.

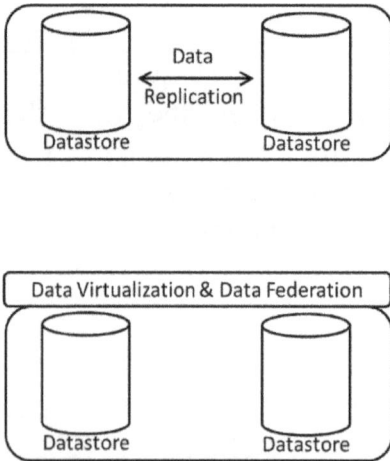

Figure 9: Data Integration

Architectural patterns for data integration can be divided into two categories: a category where data is physically copied into another location, using data replication techniques, and a category where data is accessed at the source location using data virtualization and data federation techniques. In this second category, the patterns aim to provide a holistic approach to both infra-structure and the implementtations built atop it, so that people can have a shared vision for collaboration. Hybrid combinations are possible and in fact common.

7.1.1 Data Replication

Data Replication is the copying of data from one data store to another. This is the traditional approach to integration, and still is often a knee-jerk integration solution for many software designers. In certain cases, data replication still is the best integration solution, but with an increasing business demand for low-latency, high volume and / or unstructured data analytics, other solutions than data replication have become a necessity. In integration at the business logic layer, data replication never is the best solution, but in certain cases, like MDM (master data management) might be an acceptable cheap alternative.

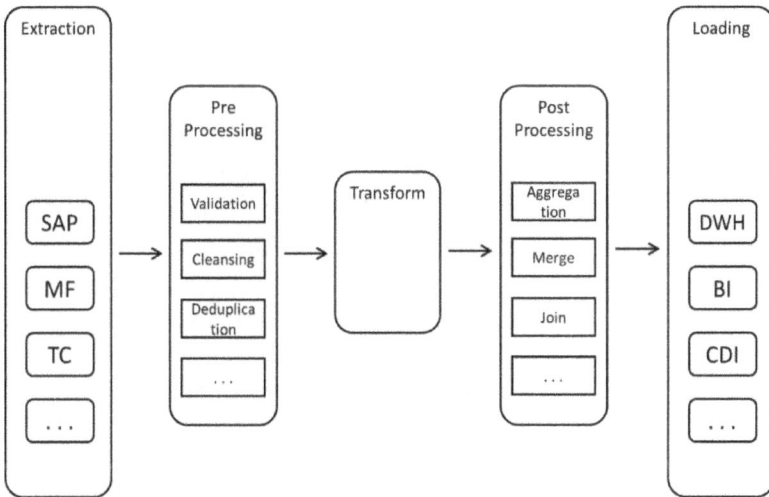

Figure 10: Data Replication

The most common architectural pattern for data replication is a broker architecture, also known as hub-and-spoke architecture. In this architecture, inter-server communication and data transfer pass through a central hub, where the communications are managed and the data may undergo some form of treatment. This hub may be anything from a vendor supplied data integration suite or a collection of home-grown routines.

There are three base patterns of data replication:

Base pattern	Description
Built-in Database replication	Database replication is offered as a capability by many database management systems. In its simplest form there is a master/slave relationship between original and copy (or copies), where the master logs updates, and the updates are then applied to the slaves. Multi-master and bi-directional database replication is also offered, but at substantially higher cost and complexity. Many databases allow replication to be executed both near real-time or batched, for example when changing log files. It is often the easiest and cheapest method of replication, but in most cases only entire databases can be replicated.
Triggered replication	A database trigger is a piece of procedural code that is executed in response to a certain event on a database table. Almost all databases support row-level BEFORE and AFTER triggers on INSERT, UPDATE and DELETE statements, and a database programmer can write procedural code associated with this trigger execute some logic to either apply a change to a copy immediately, or to collect the changes to be processed by the copy later. Like database replication, this is pretty straightforward in a master/slave relationship between original and copy (or copies), but becomes extremely complex in multi-master and bi-directional scenario's. The biggest disadvantage of this method is that it has very limited managing and monitoring support, so errors can go undetected for a long time.

| Extract & Load | Full | The required data is collected from its source, might undergo certain treatments, like validation, transformation, complementation, aggregation cleansing, filtering, and more, before being loaded into a target data store. Typically, this process is not triggered by a business event, but scheduled to execute at certain times, or at request. A full extraction often involves unnecessary overhead, since data that doesn't change, will be still be sent over and over again. In general, only data with a high change rate and a high change volume should follow this pattern. |
| | Delta | A delta replication is almost equal to a full replication. There are two notable differences: first, only the data that has been added or changed in a certain timeframe is collected. Second, in some way, the data that has been deleted in that timeframe must also be collected. Typically, this process is scheduled, or triggered by a technical event in the source, such as switching log files or journal files. In general, data with a low change rate or a low change volume should follow this pattern. It does require reference data management and a mechanism to recognize and signal deletions. |

Table 9: Data Replication base patterns

7.1.1.1 *Data replication & ETL tools*

There is a bewildering amount of commercially available tooling to configure and execute your data replication processes. Some are marketed as integration tools, others as ETL tools or business intelligence tools.

7.1.2 Data Virtualization

The term "data virtualization" may well be the most ambiguous term in contemporary IT to reach the buzz word status. While there are many different interpretations of the term, the definition on Wikipedia is not commercially tainted: *Data virtualization is an umbrella term used to describe any approach to data management that allows an application to retrieve and manipulate data without requiring technical details about the data, such as how it is formatted or where it is physically located.*

With this definition, the traditional extract, transform & load (ETL) processes can also be considered data virtualization tools. In a more restrictive interpretation, data virtualization keeps the data in place, and real-time access is given to the data source through an abstracted, logical interface.

7.1.3 Data Federation

Data federation is the aggregation of heterogeneous data from disparate sources to present it in a consistent manner through a single point of access. While some see data federation as one of the constituents of data virtualization, others see data federation as an extra, separate abstraction layer on top of data virtualization. Theoretically, data federation without data virtualization is possible.

In the end, both data virtualization and data federation are applications of the proxy design pattern (or façade pattern) that the Gang of Four described in 1994, which is exactly what the application integration layer (see Fig. 8) is too. The difference between the two is
that data virtualization and data federation present a façade to data, whereas the application integration layer presents a façade to business logic.

7.2 Application Integration

A most important, but often overlooked aspect of application integration is how to fit an application into an application network. Before we can start thinking of integration solutions, we must have delineated the responsibilities of the application, and the responsibilities of other applications in the application network, so there can be no ambiguity on which application handles which task. Just as important as avoiding overlaps in task handling is avoiding gaps in task handling: we must make sure that all potential tasks in a business process have been addressed.

To support its car sales, ACME has developed a tool called Car Configurator, that allows a client to configure a car to his personal taste and needs. Roughly, it consists of three parts: a central part, that allows the people at ACME's head office to configure the options, a public part, that allows potential clients to configure a car in a webbrowser, and a part that is available to ACME's dealerships, that allows the dealer to finalize a configuration and create a quote or order.

From an IT point of view it is a good example of a category 1 distributed system, as mentioned in chapter 4. As such, it can be considered as one single system that runs on several platforms. The system is owned by the Marketing&Sales department, but obviously it is multi-disciplinary since it is Product Development that provides the choice of options that can be configured, Product Engineering that validates the special wishes of a client, Manufacturing that can provide a production date, and Logistics that can estimate a delivery date, etc.

ACME has divided the system into three subsystems along the usage boundaries. Within each subsystem, all logic was built with microservices, while API's are provided for communication between the subsystems; these services are hosted within the Car Configurator platform, and are not accessible from outside the system.

Information from external systems is only accessible through business services. There is no user interface to maintain its local masterdata, instead the system is subscribed to events from external systems pertaining to its local masterdata. In turn, the system publishes events to external systems that are subscribed to these events. In some cases, a business service in an external system can be called to retrieve required information (i.e. *GetEstimatedDeliveryDate*). Where possible, the business services and event messages adhere to accepted standards. The business services and event message processors use the above mentioned microservices and API's, or an orchestration thereof, for processing and adapt the local vernacular to the accepted standards.

Since ACME's dealerships typically use their own software to support their processes, much of the functionality for dealerships is not only available through a portal site, but also as business services, to be called from their own software. Every external business service is addressable over both json/REST and SOAP/XML. The services and messages adhere to internationally accepted standards. The business services also use the microservices and API's or an orchestration thereof, and adapt to the international standards.

When architecting a software solution, we have a tendency to isolate the object of study from its environment, to narrow down the scope of the project, to ignore processes that lie outside the field of interest. Obviously for example, when you want to design a new ordering system, you will need business partner data, but you don't want to burden your project with business partner management support: you'll probably have an existing application to take care of that. The implicit reaction is often to get the data from another system. And this is where things often go wrong.

A requirement of a candidate application integration solution is never *"to get certain data from A to B"*. Neither is this ever the purpose of an application integration solution. The fact that a foreign visitor is able to communicate with local people does not mean the he or she is well integrated with the local people. Integration of newcomers or minorities into a society means much more than just being able to communicate. In exactly the same way, the fact that two applications can exchange information does not mean that they are well integrated. The notion of *'getting data from A to B'* is the "integration as an afterthought" approach from times long past; it is a data integration solution born out of the reconciliation of the datamodels and datastores of source and destination systems, with complete disregard for the business process(es) and information flow(s) that the solution is supposed to support.

When disregarding the underlying business processes, it is easy to fall into the trap of designing point-to-point integrations based primarily on data requirements of the destination endpoint. When designing integrations through business process modeling it becomes abundantly clear that it is not the requirements of the source or destination(s) applications that determine the content or structure of that message. The requirements of the source or destination(s) applications may only confirm the relevance of certain data elements.

Letting data requirements of a destination endpoint drive an integration design is the most serious error that is often made. This design error is often followed by the next design error: making the source endpoint responsible for gathering and sending that data. Not does this result in a point-to-point integration, it also risks making a source endpoint responsible for data of which it is not the authoritative source, or even worse, for data it doesn't have and needs to get enriched from elsewhere.

So if application integration is not about getting data exchanged between various applications or systems, then what is it? In social integration, we call a newcomer or minority well integrated when they are incorporated into the social structure of the host society, in which they participate in dialogue to achieve and maintain peaceful social relations of coexistence, collaboration and cohesion.

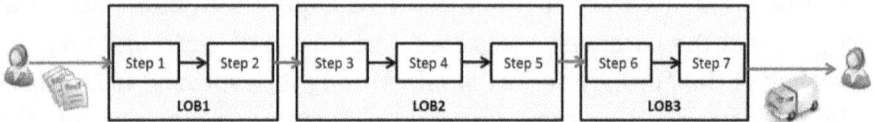

Figure 11: Integration is the support of business processes across applications, systems and platforms.

Similarly, applications are well integrated when they are incorporated into an application network, where they collaborate effectively in supporting your business processes. As we have seen, business processes are fractalic in nature, and at a high enough level, you'll need more than one enterprise application to support your business processes. Effective collaboration between these enterprise applications requires communication, harmonization, coordination and administration.

Communication	The simplistic approach to application integration limits itself to communication between enterprise applications. It concerns the technology aspect of application integration, and forms the bottom layers of the integration stack as described in the previous chapter. Whereas the protocol will enable to get data from one endpoint to another, it is the message exchange pattern that will enable effective communication between endpoints. (see also paragraph 6.5) Be aware that the protocol is not dictated by the platforms. It is the properties and requirements of an information flow and the roles of the endpoints, that determine the message exchange pattern, which in turn determines the protocol.

Harmonization	Harmonization between enterprise applications involves the structure and meaning of the information that is exchanged. The endpoints of an integration solution must be able understand each other, and to do so, they must agree on the structure of the information, and the meaning of the information. One might be tempted to adopt and apply the structure and meaning of one endpoint to the other endpoints, but this would create unwanted interdependencies and multiply complexity, thus creating brittle integration solutions. A better choice is to harmonize on a domain standard (a.k.a. canonical format or schema), thus avoiding interdependencies and lowering complexity. This harmonization can take place in the integration solution, thus safeguarding the endpoints from change.

Coordination	Coordination comprises not only the synchronization of activities between the endpoints of an integration solution, but also synchronization with other systems and integration solutions and synchronization with your business processes. Application networks that do not get their synchronization right are vulnerable to disruption. A prerequisite for coordination is clarity on who is responsible for what. You cannot coordinate a workforce of people if you do not know what each participants responsibilities are with respect to the job at hand. Similarly, you cannot achieve coordination in an integration solution without explicitly defining the responsibilities of each endpoint with regard to the information that is shared. This means that you need to know the lifecycle of each entity, element and attribute in the information that is shared, their roles in the business process, and their roles in the endpoint applications.

Administration	While technically not absolutely required to enable communication, management and monitoring of integration solutions is necessary to control the exchange of information. Whereas problems with synchronous integration solutions will show up as they occur, robust asynchronous integration solutions invariably fit invisibly between applications. Only a monitoring tool can warn of anything going wrong, often before a business process is affected, thus enabling administrators to handle potential issues before they can result in serious application network degradation. As a huge benefit of basing your integration solutions on business process models, the monitoring tool can provide invaluable insights into the performance of your running business processes.

As for enterprise applications themselves, the purpose of integration solutions must be specified as a business purpose, just as the high-level requirements of an integration must be specified as business requirements. When confronted with a *"get data from A to B"* request, it is necessary to reverse-engineer the business process model(s) in order to reverse-engineer the business requirements.

- Identify business process(es)
- Define business process(es)
- Identify business events and triggers
- Define information flow(s)

Of all the aspects that influence the choice for a certain integration solution, the most important one is which message exchange pattern (or MEP) to follow. The message exchange pattern in turn depends mainly on the information type, and on the underlying business process(es). In theory most of the Integration Stack levels, such as Message Exchange Patterns, message content and protocol are independent, which means that you should be able to use any combination. Technically, this statement is correct. In practice, however, some combinations work best, and other combinations work not at all. For instance, requesting a command is a very unlikely (but not impossible) scenario in a near real-time system.

7.2.1 Information Categories

The information type of a certain information flow depends primarily on the business process trigger and the life-cycle management of the data elements involved.

First and foremost, it is necessary to recognize that we do not exchange the objects themselves, nor should we exchange representations of them: instead we exchange information, often information about objects. Let us illustrate that with an example: when submitting an invoice from a client system, we do not send the actual invoice object, nor do we merely send the representation of an invoice to the responsible system that manages the invoice life-cycle management. Instead, we send a request message that carries the necessary information for the responsible system to create an invoice object.

To determine the information type of the message(s) to exchange, we need to establish who owns the data being exchanged. For example consider a purchasing process, where somewhere in the process purchased goods will be received, which then have to be stored or moved to the location where they are needed. The trigger for this movement of goods originates in the system supporting the purchasing process, but the execution of the movement of goods happens in a logistical system. Sending logistical data from a purchasing system to a logistical system is entirely different from sending logistical data in the reverse direction, from a logistical system to a purchasing system. Since the purchasing system does not own the information flows associated with movement of goods, but the logistical system does, the purchasing system should not send commands to the logistical system to register or execute movement of goods. Instead it should only send logistical requests to the logistical system, where in turn, the logistical system should send notifications whether it has or has not registered or executed the movement of goods.

To be able to choose the right message exchange pattern, the right granularity and the right payload, it is important to establish the role that the involved systems play with regard to life-cycle management of the involved data elements. Most important in this respect is the correct understanding of the term "master data".

Wikipedia: "Master data represents the business objects which are agreed on and shared across the enterprise. [. . .] **Master Data** is a *single source* of basic business data used across **multiple** systems, applications, and/or processes." Whereas this is a perfectly valid definition of the term "master data", it is not the most convenient definition for the purpose of interface design, because it does not distinguish entities (business objects) from attributes, but emphasizes the *"single source"* of the data. The best way to interpret the term master data is to regard it as *"data* originating *from* a *master"*. The control of the lifecycle of master data lies outside the boundaries of the solution.

For this book, we consider the term "data" in the broadest sense, to represent entities, elements, attributes, relations, etc. We distinguish three categories of data, their definitions depend on the role the data play in the business processes.

- *Process data* a.k.a. transactional data or operational data: the data that does get actively created or changed within the business processes within your domain. Typically, process data has a high create- or change-rate. Example: Invoices.

- **Master data** is the data that does take part in your business processes, but is not actively created or changed within your business processes. Typically, master data has a low create- or change-rate. Example: Business Partners. However, high change rates can occur, for example part pricing or exchange rates.

- **Reference data** is the data that is referenced in your processes, but does not take part in your business processes. Typically, reference data has a very low create- or change-rate. Example: Country names.

Note that *category* is not a fixed attribute of a data element; it rather is the role that a data element plays in a specific situation. In what category a specific entity or attribute falls, depends on the domain within which you address the entity or attribute; thus a *"Product"* can be a process entity in the *Manufacturing* domain, but can be a master entity in the *Sales* or *AfterSales* domains. Please take note that although some entity in a particular domain may be considered a master entity, not all of its attributes need to be master attributes. For example, the *"current stock level"* may be implemented as an attribute of the *"Product"* entity. In the *Logistics* domain, the *"Product"* entity might be a master entity, but the *"current stock level"* attribute is certainly a process attribute.

There is a fourth category of data: metadata. We distinguish between metadata about the exchange, and metadata about information. The latter is rarely exchanged between applications or systems. A potential scenario might be sending information through key-value-pairs, which by itself is rarely a good choice. The key-value-pair might be annotated with a type attribute, denoting how the value is to be treated, e.g. like a date or a decimal.

Metadata to the exchange, refers to the exchange itself. An example is a language code to specify the language in which a response should be sent.

It is important to establish for each attribute, within each domain, its data category and its authoritative source.

7.2.2 Local copy

Theoretically, since master data is not created or changed within your business processes, you would not need to have your own data store for master data, for you could retrieve the information from an outside source that has the information available. However, to satisfy performance or integrity, or even legal requirements, you will probably want to have one or more local copies of the master data. Obviously, the same goes for reference data; you could retrieve it when and as needed from an outside data source, but normally you will have one or more local copies.

Every entity or attribute has some form of lifecycle, and there is always someone or something responsible for creating, managing and retiring an entity or attribute. This someone or something is often called the "master" of the entity or attribute, but since this term conflicts with our notion of master data, the term "authoritative source" will be used throughout this book. The authoritative source for a company's VAT number is the government, the authoritative source for a company's telephone number is its telecom provider. The authoritative source for a part is its manufacturer, and the authoritative source for countrycodes is the ISO-3166 standard.

> An authoritative source is the system or organization that governs the lifecycle of a business entity or business attribute.

So, an authoritative source is the system or organization that governs the lifecycle of a business entity or attribute. Typically, you own or control the authoritative sources for your process data, and you do not own or control the authoritative sources for your master and reference data. Since in most situations, with respect to performance, integrity and other requirements, it may be impractical to directly access authoritative source systems for your master and reference data, you will typically maintain a local copy of these master and reference data. Of course, in some cases the reverse is true: it will be impractical to maintain a local copy of real-time stock-exchange share values with respect to the highly volatile nature of the information.

If you have more than one local copy of master or reference data, it makes sense to promote one of the local copies to play the role of local authoritative source. This local authoritative system can vary from a very simple copy or subset copy of a single external authoritative source without any business logic (e.g. SupportedLanguages), to a very large system combining several external authoritative sources and adding business logic to support local attributes, relations and processes (e.g. Business Partner Management).

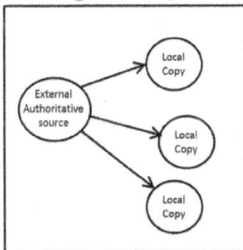

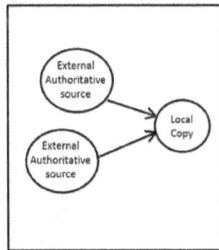

Figure 12a: Local Copies   Figure 12b: Local Copy   Figure 12c: Local Authoritative Source

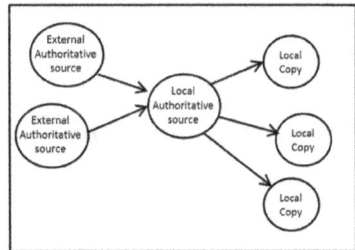

The local authoritative source plays the role of authoritative source to all internal systems; However, in the communication with its external sources, it plays the role of slave. A classic example is

Business Partner Management, for which you might have a dedicated solution as local authoritative source. You cannot create a new business partner, you can only register a new business partner. You cannot create a new address or a VAT number for the business partner, although you can create a new local ID and authorizations for the business partner. This makes *"address"* and *"VAT number"* master data, and makes *"local ID"* and *"authorizations"* process data. For some business applications it can make sense to have a local copy of business partner data, you might think of an *Ordering* service or an *Invoicing* service. These business applications play the role of slave of the business partner management solution. They are not allowed to manage the lifecycle of a business partner or any of its attributes known in the local authoritative source. They are however allowed to manage the lifecycle of a business partner and any of its attributes in the local copy within their own domain, but obviously should do so in accordance with the local authoritative source. For example you cannot create a new supplier in your purchasing system's local copy of business partners, but you can copy a new supplier from the authoritative source of business partners. Similarly, the purchasing system can delete a supplier from its local copy of business partners, but it cannot delete a supplier from the authoritative source of business partners; what it can do is send a notification to the authoritative source that is has removed the supplier. It is up to the authoritative source how to handle this notification. If your purchasing system can allow certain privileges to certain suppliers, it can add these attributes to its local copy of suppliers, and be the authoritative source for these attributes.

Let's revisit the example of page 29, where we need to register the support level for each customer, maybe in the CRM solution, maybe in the support management solution. The first question that needs to be answered is, who is the owner of the data element *"SupportLevel"*, followed by the question, what is the authoritative source of this data element. Then you can decide where to register the element. Note that although usually data elements are registered in their authoritative source system, this does not necessarily need to be true: you can have one system store a certain data element, and make another system responsible for its lifecycle management. In terms of the example, you can register the *"SupportLevel"* in the CRM solution, and make the support management solution responsible for its lifecycle management vice-versa.

Some examples from the ACME business processes to illustrate the concept of authoritative source:

- The Sales process is the authoritative source for a virtual car defined as a set of features and options.
- The Engineering process is the authoritative source for a virtual car defined as a set of components.
- The Manufacturing process is the authoritative source for a physical car assembled from a set of components.
- The AfterSales process is the authoritative source for a physical car after it has been delivered to a dealer or customer.

During the delivery of a car it receives a licenseplate number from the vehicle registration authority (VRA). That makes the VRA the external authoritative source for licenseplate numbers. An AfterSales process will register the licenseplate number in its datastore, which makes the system implementing this AfterSales process a local authoritative source for licenseplate numbers.

As stated above, the authoritative source for a car to be ordered in terms of features and options is the Sales process. The set of valid available combinations of features and options however is an entirely different responsibility for which not the Sales process but the Engineering process is the authoritative source.

Whether information is sent from or to an authoritative source is a decisive factor in choosing name, content and MEP. Messages are sent *from* an authoritative source in the form of notifications. Notifications suggest that no response is expected. Messages are sent *to* an authoritative source in the form of requests. Requests imply that a response is expected.

7.2.3 Choosing message exchange patterns

Roughly, application integration solutions can be categorized into two categories, master data integration and process integration. Designing your application integration solutions to fall neatly into one of these categories will allow for stable, straightforward solutions. Application integration solutions that do not fit smoothly into one of these categories tend to be awkward and often do not meet your business process requirements well.

7.2.3.1 *Master data integration*

Per definition, life cycle management of master data lies outside your area of competence; if it would lie within your area of competence, it wouldn't be master data, it would be process data. Data traffic between an authoritative source and a local copy is fundamentally one-way: from the authoritative source to the local copy. Basically, the flow of information from authoritative source to local copy involves only master data or reference data, never process data. The flow can be implemented technically or functionally. The technical solution is by some replication mechanism; the disadvantage of replication is its rigidity. The functional solution has the benefits of allowing business rules and policies to be applied to the transfer.

A technical solution by replication is a tightly coupled point-to-point dependency between authoritative source and local copy. If implemented at the datastore level, for example through mirroring or log shipping, it can be very efficient. When implemented as exports from the authoritative source, and imports in the local copy, it is not only very inefficient, it's playing Russian roulette with the continuity of your business process support. Either way, all technical solutions are business process agnostic, so business rules and policies are difficult to impossible to apply, and receivers will miss out on important business context information.

The functional solution depends on the business trigger: is it an event in the authoritative source, or is it the request of the local copy that triggers the data transfer? In the first case (an event in the authoritative source), the Publish & Subscribe message exchange pattern is used, where the authoritative source publishes notifications that it has registered in its authoritative datastore, and the local copy subscribes to these notifications, and registers them in its local datastore.

In the second case (at request of the local copy), the Request/Response or Solicit/Response message exchange pattern is used, where the local copy requests certain information from the authoritative source to register in its local datastore. Imagine figures 12b and 12c: A message from one authority might make it necessary for the local copy to receive information from another authority. In this case, the local copy may send a request message to the other authority.

In the case of an external authoritative source you are dependent on the services that the external party can offer. Often, the Publish & Subscribe pattern is not available. A good strategy would be to introduce a local authoritative source that can reconstruct business triggers from received data, and offer a Publish & Subscribe solution to the internal clients.

Master data traffic between a local copy and a Line-Of-Business application that is not the authoritative source for that local copy is also fundamentally one-way: from the local copy to the Line-Of-

Business application. The most common solution uses the Request/Response or Solicit/Response message exchange pattern, but a Publish & Subscribe message exchange pattern is also allowed.

7.2.3.2 *Process Data Integration*

Process Data Integration takes place between Line-Of-Business systems. It's these LOB systems that support the execution of the business processes, and that is why the integration solutions between LOB systems should reflect the information flow between these business processes, not only in information content, but also in behavioral aspects. The business event and the associated information flow will guide you to a suitable message exchange pattern and message design. If an integration solution between two (or more) LOB systems cannot be related to an information flow between business processes, or the triggering cannot be related to a business event, then a redesign of the solution is essential.

Unfortunately, often LOB systems are of-the-shelf ERP packages that not always provide the integration endpoints that are necessary to allow a suitable message exchange pattern or message design. If this is the case, the best course of action would be to put a service layer proxy in front of the ERP package that does support the suitable message exchange patterns and message designs. If the service layer proxy is not an option, a substandard integration solution based on best effort is unavoidable.

As stated earlier, information from an authoritative source to a local copy or client, when initiated by the authoritative source, is preferably transferred using event notifications. Note that an event notification represents a business event that has been signaled by an authoritative source, and as such per definition is correct. If, for whatever reason, a local copy or client cannot process an event notification, then the local copy or client must handle the situation, never the authoritative source. The local copy or client must not send some sort of feedback or error message back to the originating authoritative source, since the event notification per definition is correct. This also means that the Fire & Forget or Publish & Subscribe message exchange pattern must be used.

7.2.4 Transport protocol

The business services on the integration layer are addressed over a transport protocol, and there is no dependency between service and protocol other than that the protocol must support the message exchange pattern that the service implements. One of the most important aspects of business services is interoperability, that is the ability of different information technology systems and software to communicate, exchange and use data and information from each other. Apart from functional interoperability, the ability to understand each other's information, there is technical interoperability (sometimes called foundational interoperability), the ability to get the information across. This is where transport protocol comes in: SOAP/XML over http is a transport protocol that is widely supported over many operating systems and programming languages, and would be an excellent choice for interoperable services, but it inherently cannot support 100% reliability, so for reliable message exchange patterns another protocol must be found.

Since there are no other dependencies, there is nothing stopping you from defining more than one protocol to a given service. It requires that you separate business logic from protocol (which is always a good principle). For example, you might create a service with three endpoints so it can receive event messages over three different protocols, one endpoint using named pipes for messages from clients that reside on the same machine as the service, one endpoint using AMQP for messages from clients that require high reliability, and one http(s) endpoint for messages from simple clients for who 100% reliability is not a requirement.

7.2.5   Message design

In a top-down approach, where business processes and their information flows are iteratively decomposed to lower level business processes, the message definition is a product of the information flow analysis. In practice however, we are often confronted with a bottom-up approach, where we need to reverse-engineer the business processes and their associated information flows, or worse, we cannot relate the integration solution to a business process. Either way, whether you are defining information flows for business processes, or designing message contracts for integration solutions, the most important aspect is coherence. A measurement for coherence is cohesion, and cohesion largely determines autonomy and granularity. The importance of cohesion was already recognized in the 60ies (Yourdon, Constantine i.a.). The following types of cohesion were distinguished:

- Coincidental cohesion is when parts of a service are grouped arbitrarily; the only relationship between the parts is that they have been grouped together (e.g. a "Utilities" service).
- Logical cohesion is when parts of a service are grouped because they belong to the same general category though they are different by nature (e.g. a Math service grouping all kinds of mathematical routines).
- Temporal cohesion is when parts of a service are grouped by when they are related in time (e.g. an exception handling service which closes open files, creates an error log, and notifies the user).
- Procedural cohesion is when parts of a service are grouped because they are related only by sequence, but the activities are unrelated (e.g. a service which checks file permissions and then opens a file).
- Informational cohesion (sometimes called communicational cohesion) is when parts of a service are grouped because

they operate on the same entities (e.g. a service which operates on a business partner entity).

- Sequential cohesion is when parts of a service are grouped because the output from one part is the input to another part like an assembly line (e.g. a service which opens a file, reads data, processes data and closes the file).
- Functional cohesion is when parts of a service are grouped because they all contribute to a single well-defined process-related task of the service (e.g. a PurchaseOrderConfirmation).

Be aware that the recurring phrase *"parts of a service are grouped"* imply a bottom-up design approach, where a top-down approach would be much more appropriate, and would help avoiding pitfalls with regard to cohesion. While functional cohesion is considered the most desirable type of cohesion for a service, it may not always be achievable. There are circumstances where informational cohesion is the highest level of cohesion that can be attained. The types of cohesion are listed in order of desirability; coincidental cohesion should be avoided most since it leads to unnecessary tight coupling, functional cohesion should be sought most, since it leads to right granularity and loose coupling. A good understanding of the lifecycle of data elements and attributes (where are they created, modified and deleted, by whom, in what processes) is indispensable for attaining the right cohesion in message design.

Within informational cohesion you should consider subgrouping: an entity may have many attributes, and you may want to create subgroups of attributes. The criteria by which you want to subgroup may vary: they might be functional, for example subgrouping attributes related to addresses, prices, or lifecycle. The criteria might also be more technical, for example subgrouping attributes that tend to change often versus attributes that tend to change rarely if ever.

Sometimes the distinction is quite subtle. Consider the following situation: before a car leaves the factory floor, the axle pressures must be weighed and registered. For this to happen, the car drives over a weighbridge, where each axle pressure is weighed individually. One possibility is to define an *"AxlePressureWeighed"* event message, that contains the identification and measured weight of one axle. E.g. a car with 2 axles will generate two messages. An alternative possibility is to define an aggregated *"AxlePressuresWeighed"* event message, that contains the identification of a car and the measured weight of each of the axles. In this case, you will also need some aggregator service to combine the individual measurements into the aggregated message.

Also before leaving the factory floor, several fluid holders must be partially filled, such as fuel, brake fluid, gear oil etc. and the amounts must be registered. From a technical viewpoint, it is tempting to define one message that reports all measurements. However, from a business process viewpoint, filling and measuring fuel, brake fluid and gear oil are three, maybe even six, different processes, that do not have to occur at or around the same time. When combining these measurements a dependency would be introduced that in reality doesn't exist.

Avoid "snapshot" integration in application integration; a "snapshot" contains the state of an instance of an entity or set of entities. Consider an entity *"Order"* with an attribute *"status"* that can have one of four possible values: *"Received"*, *"Rejected"*, *"Confirmed"* or *"Cancelled"*. Instead of sending snapshots of the *"Order"* entity when the *"status"* attribute changes, it is much better to publish *"OrderReceived"*, *"OrderRejected"*, *"OrderConfirmed"* or *"OrderCancelled"* event messages when that business event occurs. These event messages are good examples of functional cohesion, whereas "snapshot" integration is a form of informational cohesion.

Note that "delta" files also fall into the "snapshot" category. They do not contain event notifications, but snapshots of entities, or worse, snapshots of data, that have changed in a particular period, usually since the previous time a "delta" file was generated. As stated before, a better approach is to send the business event notification(s) that led to these changes. If this cannot be achieved designing the information to mimic business event notification(s) is an acceptable alternative, to be preferred above "snapshots".

There are very few business processes where "snapshot" integration is a good choice. One potential example is when one or more of your primary business processes use master data that, according to business rules have a fixed validity, for example daily exchange rates. Then a scheduled solution for gathering the master data might be contemplated; for the given example you might implement a solution that gathers the daily exchange rates once every day. This is one of few cases where "snapshot" integration might be a suitable choice in a primary business process. Otherwise, "snapshot" integration should be considered only for data gathering processes, for example data gathering processes for business intelligence.

> As an illustration for a valid "snapshot" integration solution: For its daily exchange rates ACME has a scheduled task that every day calls a service at the World Bank Group to retrieve the exchange rates for that day as determined by this institution. This is stored in a local datastore which serves as the local authoritative source to the rest of the applications network.

Even if business process requirements might seem to warrant an integration solution based on scheduled downloads ("snapshot" integration), it still often is a bad idea. For example, imagine a production company where at the start of each year new product types may be released. You might contemplate creating a yearly scheduled download of valid product types, and uploading this into various local copies. Using this approach would mean losing very valuable information, because each local copy now has to compare the new set of values against the old set of values, to determine which new product types have been released, which product types were retired, which were changed and which haven't changed. Much better would it be to have the authoritative source send a set of event messages like *"ProductTypeReleased"*, *"ProductType-Changed"* and *"ProductTypeRetired"*. The benefits of this approach are less data traffic, easier message routing, better process support, improved resilience, increased responsiveness and better monitoring. If for some reason the authoritative source only supports "snapshot" integration, a good strategy would be to introduce a service layer that receives the "snapshot" information and generates the desired event messages, thus consolidating the logic to recreate business events into one place.

ACME has a large part of its business processes supported by ERP and legacy applications. These ERP and legacy applications use snapshot data integration techniques for integration solutions. As a consequence, each night a large amount of data is extracted from legacy databases, and sent to various destinations to be imported into other applications.

Some of these exports are "full exports", meaning that every night the whole dataset will be extracted, even if nothing has changed, and that every client will receive and process the whole dataset, also even if nothing has changed. Performance and responsiveness of involved applications is severely affected during this export/import stage, and becoming an issue with an increasing round-the-clock demand.

Some of the ERP and legacy database tables have a "LastModified" attribute, which enables ACME to fine-tune the daily extraction process to extract only those records that have been modified since the last extraction. This limits the amount of data being exported and imported and is a huge improvement over the full export/import, but it still does not provide the context for the change.

In some cases, ACME was able to transform these delta-files into business events. This led to improved reliability and less down-time but still cannot deliver the same benefits that a pure event messaging architecture can.

The registration of an event is not the business event itself: Imagine a typical HR process where employee John Smith gets promoted to manager by the first day of the next month. In a real-time environment you might be tempted to publish this event immediately to interested clients. But doing so would require all clients to invest in business logic that allows beforehand registration of a future state. In most cases this is not a viable option, or at least an expensive solution.

In fact, the beforehand registration of this promotion in the HR system is not the business event of HR promotion, it's merely a registration event. The promotion itself is a business event that will occur at midnight at the start of the first day of the next month, and that is the event that should be published. So instead of real-time signaling HR registration events, it makes much more sense to have a daily batch-process that collects all changes that have started that day, and publish these as event messages. Particularly note that this is not "snapshot" integration; the traditional "snapshot" approach, which produces exports or executes imports of snapshot data on a scheduled basis, is pernicious and can easily be avoided.

Create, Update and Delete activities on datasets are also not business events: Imagine you have a dataset containing car information, the cars having attributes such as *"RegistrationPlate"*, *"InsuranceNr"*, and *"EngineNr"*. The application with which you maintain this car dataset has a GUI where you can enter values for these attributes. You might be tempted to publish a "Vehicle*Changed*" event whenever one of these attributes is changed, or even worse, schedule a batch process that harvests changes on the *"Vehicle"* entity in the dataset that has taken place since the last harvest (so-called delta-files). These are not business events, and it only ensures a mismatch or discontinuity in your processes.
Instead, changing the *"RegistrationPlate"* attribute is an action in the car registration process, changing the *"InsuranceNr"* attribute is an action in the car insurance process, and changing the *"EngineNr"* attribute is an action in the process of swapping an engine in a workshop. It is these event messages that should be published, with names like *"VehicleRegistered"*, *"VehicleInsured"* or *"EngineSwap-Executed"*. The benefits of this approach are the same as mentioned before: less data traffic, easier message routing, better process support, improved resilience, increased responsiveness and better monitoring.
When working bottom-up, designing event messages by reverse-engineering business processes, the granularity of an event is not

always self-evident. Depending on various criteria, the granularity of an *"<entity>Changed"* event may be too coarse, while the granularity of an *"<attribute>Changed"* event may be too fine. Consider an action where the zipcode of a business partner gets changed. Throwing an *"BusinessPartnerZipcodeChanged"* event would be too fine-grained, throwing an *"BusinessPartnerChanged"* event would be too coarse-grained. A better choice would to group all address related events to an *"BusinessPartnerAddressChanged"* event; this is a nice concise and functional grouping of attributes, with the additional benefits of allowing routing and filtering.

ACME has an OrderIntake process, where one of the subprocesses is a CreditCheck of the potential customer. Depending on the business rules that have been set for the CreditCheck evaluation, the CreditCheck function may need a lot of information in order to be able to perform its evaluation, for example the name of one or more external agencies involved in the check. But it is not the task, nor the responsibility of the OrderIntake process to provide all of this information. The OrderIntake process only provides information directly related to the incoming order, all other information that the CreditCheck evaluation requires, it will have to gather from other sources. The message from the OrderIntake process to the CreditCheck evaluation can contain only data directly related to the incoming order, but not a reference to the external agencies.

Use special care when exchanging coded or keyed data elements. If the code or key of a data element adheres to a global or generally acknowledged standard, such as ISO or DIN, then it is perfectly OK to use that code or key as-is. You may consider assigning a namespace reflecting the standard to the data element. For example:

```
<Country xmlns:iso3166="http://www.itu.int/tML/tML-ISO-
3166">
   <iso3166:CountryCode>UK</iso3166:CountryCode>
</Country>
```

If data elements are coded or keyed using a proprietary standard, exchanging these proprietary codes and keys by themselves amount to a functional tight coupling: at least one system must know about the internal proprietary codes and keys of another system. In doing so, they lose their autonomy. Instead, an enumeration or a keyvaluepair should be used. To make the right choice, several aspects must be taken into consideration. One aspect is the stability of the list of codes or keys for a certain data element. If a new code or key is rarely or never added or deleted, and the list of codes or keys is not too long, then an enumeration is an obvious choice. Another aspect is the scope of impact: if adding a new code or key or deleting one has functional meaning for most or all clients, then too an enumeration is a good choice. The third aspect is technical; if adding or deleting keys and codes does not break contracts, then an enumeration is still a good choice. In all other cases, a fallback to a keyvaluepair is needed, where a pairing of key (or code) and value (it's functional meaning) is transferred. For example:

```
<ErrorSeverity code="4">Critical</ErrorSeverity>
```

Another aspect to consider when establishing data contracts outside business process context is how direction of an information flow affects content. In general, identifying data elements can be sent in all directions for reference, all non-identifying data elements should be sent only from authoritative source to client. For example, when sending in a PurchaseOrder, you can fill in all details of the buyer, since you are the authoritative source of this information. For each item in your PO, you can specify the seller's itemnumber and name, since they can be considered identifying attributes. You may specify an itemprice, since you are the authoritative source for specifying what price you are prepared to pay, but you should not specify the listprice, since the seller is the authoritative source for this data element.

7.2.6 Interoperability

In paragraph 7.2.4. we discussed technical interoperability, the ability to exchange data, which is addressed at the protocol level. Just as important as technical interoperability is functional interoperability. The basic level of functional interoperability is structural interoperability, the ability to process information, that is, to recognize the structure or format of information; it defines the syntax of the information exchange. Defining the structure for a specific information exchange is a form of functional tight coupling, which cannot entirely be avoided, but it can be mitigated by using data contracts based on *canonical data models*.

There are many different definitions of the term *canonical data model*, and most of them are wrong. A canonical data model models the information involved in your business processes in a common structure and format that is recognizable for all applications supporting your business processes. It is not, as many suggest, a reconciliation of your various data models, comparable to the artificial Esperanto language as a go-between for translations between various languages, although it does function as a go-between language. The focus on business process information encourages functional loose coupling by application of the "implementation hiding" principle. A good example of the "implementation hiding" principle is placing a phone call: it is a service that your telecom provider provides, and you as a client know how to use it: You dial a number (or select a name, and your phone dials the number for you) and as if by magic, somewhere in the world, another phone goes ringing, and if it gets picked up, you can start a conversation. Only, there is no magic, it is the internal workings of the service that you do not need to know, probably not even want to know, that creates the connection, but for the business process (the phone call) between the client and the telecom provider it's completely irrelevant. In the same way, canonical data models must be based on the business process data flows, and you should never allow internal implementation details of the service nor any client to simmer through into the canonical data model.

Some people confuse a canonical data model with an *enterprise wide* data model. These are not the same! For example, if you are a manufacturing organization, your *ProductDevelopment* department will have a very different view of the *Product* entity than the *Manufacturing* and *Marketing&Sales* departments. The same will be true for their business processes, and for the information flowing through these business processes. You cannot create a model that will fit all business processes, but you can create various views on the same enterprise entities. In the given example, you will probably create a different canonical data model for each of the three main business processes. Just make sure that they are not in conflict with each other, and that together they may present a holistic view on the business entity. If you so wish, you might call this holistic view an *enterprise wide* data model. And remember, these canonical and enterprise wide data models are defined for the purpose of operational integration. For other purposes, for instance Business Intelligence, you will need to define other models, which may be similar, but need not be identical.

The difference between canonical data model and domain model is less obvious. You might argue that a canonical data model is a subset of the domain model, providing only the structure and format aspects of a domain model. This argument only fails for processes that cross domain boundaries, which, *ipso facto*, is the main area of interest for integration architecture. Still, domain models are an essential prerequisite for building canonical models for your business processes, but care must be taken that information private to the domain does not get exposed to outside the domain. E.g. *Cost Center* is a typical accounting term referring to the internal administration of Financial business processes, and will be present in the Finance domain model as such. But as it is internal to the financial processes, it must not be exposed in data contracts to clients outside the financial domain.

Another essential distinction that is rarely understood, is the difference between canonical model and data contract. As explained in previous paragraphs, integration services exchange messages, not objects. Canonical models model object-types (entities), not message-types. Data contracts define message-types, not object-types. Obviously, for integration services we need data contracts, not canonical models! To reach our goal of functional interoperability, we must define the data contract on the basis of a canonical model. This not only ensures functional interoperability, but also secures horizontal and vertical consistency (cross-boundary and cross-discipline), eases maintenance and promotes reuse.

Business processes do not exist in isolation, the business processes in your organization are entwined with the business processes in other organizations. Ordering, invoicing, delivery, claim handling, these are examples of business processes that cross organizational boundaries. Integration services that support these business processes will need to use data contracts that are understood by all involved organizations. This realization resulted in the creation of information exchange standards like EDI and SWIFT already in the 70ies of the previous century. With the explosion of information exchange potential due to the phenomenal increase in internet resources, a great many new standardization initiatives have seen the light. Some standardization efforts, like ebXML and OAGIS, are generic in nature, others, like HL7, LEDES and SBML, are branch, domain or industry-specific. It makes sense, when establishing your canonical models, to adopt a global standard. It even makes sense to adopt different global standards depending on the business domain. An often heard complaint about these global messaging standards is that they are too large, unwieldy and cumbersome to work with. An easy escape is to create your canonical model on a subset of a global standard, that contains only the elements and attributes that are relevant to your business process.

In practice, you'll notice that sometimes legacy services require data elements or attributes that are not foreseen in the canonical data models. Obviously, since these elements or attributes are missing, they are not relevant to the business process, but only relevant to the legacy service implementation. The fundamental principles of service autonomy, implementation hiding and separation of concerns dictate that you do not allow internal details of a service to pollute the data contract. The solution is to either alter the service to honor data contracts as required by the business process that they support, or create a *"wrapper"* service that takes care of the internal details. If neither option is viable, as a last resort you can adapt the data contract. Under no circumstance should you alter the underlying canonical models with the offending details.

Interoperability in .Net

Services require a defined contract between the service and the client(s). This contract describes the data and operations provided by the service and any expectations over their use. These contracts are supposed to be platform-independent and fully interoperable

---

constructs that can be consumed by any client. To ensure this independency and interoperability, the software that implements these services must adhere to these contracts explicitly.

The idea of contract first development was first proposed as part of the Eiffel programming language in the mid-1980s and is a big part in most Java based frameworks. It's never been a big part of the .Net world as it has always been built around code-based abstraction of service definitions. The classical asmx web services of .Net versions 2.0 and lower utilized tooling (the *xsd.exe* class generator and *XmlSerializer*) to render web services that produced the desired results.

The primary drawback in WCF has always been the lack of reliable tooling for contract-first development as WCF is completely orientated towards code-first development. The default tooling provided for .Net 3.0 and onwards was the svcutil.exe for class generation and *DataContractSerializer* for xml (de)serializing. Both do not produce the desired results. To honor contract-first development it requires that the programmer uses the "old" xsd.exe class generator and changes the default serializer for each project into the *XmlSerializer*.

We had to wait for the introduction of .Net 4.5 and Visual Studio 2012 for Microsoft to introduce the *Contract-First* tool. This tool provides a dialogue where you can, among other things, select the desired class generator and serializer.

So to ensure interoperability of your services in .Net requires to use one of three possible approaches:
- create classical .asmx web services.
- create WCF web services, manually using *xsd.exe* and *XmlSerializer*.
- create WCF web services selecting *xsd.exe* and *XmlSerializer* in the *Contract-First* tool.

The advanced level of functional interoperability is semantic interoperability, the ability to understand the exact meaning of each other's information. The elements and attributes in your data models should have meaningful names, but there is a limit as to how precise you can match the name of an element or attribute to its meaning. E.g. consider a data element called "PartsAvailable": does it represent the number of parts that is available on the shelf in the warehouse, or is it that number, from which the number of ordered parts is already subtracted? Semantic interoperability must be documented, centrally in a data architecture repository, or locally as comment in the definition.

One often overseen aspect is non-functional interoperability, where service and client must be able to meet the same non-functional requirements. E.g. if a service is not available during a maintenance window, and a client demands 24/7 availability, there is a mismatch that must be resolved. Obviously, service level management plays an important role here.

7.2.7 Batch or Scheduled Processing

In the early years of enterprise automation, batch processing was the *de facto* standard, primarily because the existing technology at that time was not equipped to facilitate real-time processing. With the technologies available to us today, this is no longer a reason to indulge in batch processing solution.
Batch processing may still be a valid choice, but only if the involved business processes are batch oriented. Some examples of scheduled or batch-oriented business-processes are:

- Daily collection of orders to create and send invoices
- Periodical payments file to the bank

- Daily personnel changes becoming active that day
- Yearly tax statements

Typically, but not necessarily, these business-processes are end-to-end batch-oriented, meaning the whole business process, from starting point at the source to the end point at the destination(s) is batch-oriented. Although technically it is easy to allow batch processing tasks to use message oriented integration services, in practice this is fraught with danger: in synchronous scenarios it can mean overloading services in such a way that it may lead to complete infrastructure failure, similar to a DoS (denial-of-service) attack. In asynchronous scenarios, which are much more robust, it will result in serious performance degradation: the integration infrastructure is idle for most of the time, punctuated by short bursts of overloading, not only degrading its own performance, but also degrading the performance of other interfaces.

As with other business processes, batch business processes need a business event to be triggered; if a batch process cannot be tied to a business event, then the process is probably a technical solution, not the implementation of a business process. The distinction becomes tricky when the business event is time-based: for example a daily invoice run. The difference here is, that it is a business decision to execute the business process with a certain periodicity, in the given example, to execute the invoicing process once daily.

With respect to content, within application integration the same rules apply for message oriented and batch oriented solutions: the sets of data should preferably contain event-type messages, submit-type and object-type messages are also quite common. Refrain from using "records" or "composite records"; while these may be acceptable in a data integration environment, in an application integration environment this type of content creates unwanted dependencies and potential operational issues. Other message types (see also paragraph 6.7) may be considered with care.

7.2.8 Applicability

Table 10 lists the most common application integration scenario's.

	Information Type	Source	Destination	Naming	Pattern
Push	Process Event	LOB	any	<Entity><Verb> (*past participle*) *e.g. PartsOrderReceived*	Fire&Forget Publish / Subscribe
Pull	Process Data	LOB	any	Get<QualifiedEntity> List<QualifiedEntities> *e.g. GetPartsInvoice*	Solicit / Response Request / Response
Push	Action	LOB	authoritative source	<Verb><Entity> *e.g. SubmitPartsOrder*	Solicit / Response Request / Response
Push	Master data	authoritative source	local copy	<Entity><Verb> (*past participle*) *e.g. BusinessPartnerCreated*	Fire&Forget Publish / Subscribe
Pull	Master data Reference data	authoritative source	any	Get<QualifiedEntity> List<QualifiedEntities> *e.g. ListSupportedLanguages GetPartsPricing*	Solicit / Response Request / Response
Batch	Process data: Set of entities, e.g. monthly payments from salary run Set of events, e.g. HR changes that have become effective.	LOB	LOB	<Entities> <Entity> </Entity> </Entities> *e.g.* <Items> <Item> < . . ./> </Item> </Items>	Publish / Subscribe Scheduled MFT

Table 10; Real-time interfacing. N.B. in Request/Response and Solicit/Response scenario's the "Source" column denotes the system that is the source of the response; the "Destination" column denotes the system that is the receiver of the response.

Below are a few simple design rules-of-thumb that may aid you in improving your integration efforts:

- Push information from an authoritative source in the form of events.
- Pull information from an authoritative source in the form of requests.
- Invoke an action by an authoritative system in the form of a submit.
- Do not send commands, unless you are sending from a workflow or choreography / orchestration engine.
- Make sure service clients do not need to know any internal details of a service.
- Do not use data replication patterns in application integration, unless the involved business process is scheduled or batch oriented.
- If you see an element or attribute named *"state"* or *"status"*, make sure you are not creating a snapshot integration where you should use an event-based integration instead.
- If you see a servicename or a methodname starting with *"create"*, *"update"* or *"delete"*, make sure you're designing a business service, not a data access module.

7.2.9 Pagination

The loose coupling principle dictates that we should not create dependencies between client and server buy building or holding state between interactions. But what patterns can be followed when a client wants to consume a service that may return an open ended number of 'rows'? Some message queueing protocols have a maximum message size that is small enough to make this a concrete issue. GUI applications solve this with pagination. Pagination requires that the server holds the data and that the client request the data in chunks. Can we use this pattern for business services?

Consider building a RESTful web service; the principles of REST tell us that a URL should represent a resource. So the URL http://myApi/items/123 will represent the item with an ID of 123. Following that pattern, then http://myApi/items/ should represent all items. But what if there are thousands of items? The response could become too large, as that would really upset consumers on a slow connection. A way to solve this, as you'll see often used by web applications, is through query string pagination, e.g. http://myApi/items?offset=60&limit=30, which means 'starting from item 60, give me the next 30 items'. This allows the consumer a fine control over the pagination of the response to suit their needs. So does this solve the issue?

When paging through the items of a result set, it is probably important to not skip a row or duplicate a row. Probably too, while the client is paging through the result set, data may be inserted and deleted at any time. Also, the sequence of items in the result set may be altered by external causes. The only way to ensure completeness and consistency over the paginated result set is by creating the result set upon an initial request, and referring to this result set on subsequent requests. But this violates the rule of not keeping state between interactions. This rule exists with good reason: statefulness can compromise the availability of a service, deteriorate its performance, and undermine its scalability potential.

The recommendation therefore is:
- Do not use pagination on a service contract.
- If there is no way to avoid pagination on a service contract, carefully consider and evaluate two equally bad alternatives before making a choice: either create a stateful service and

risk availability, scalability and performance issues or accept potential incompleteness or inconsistency of the result set.

7.3 Versioning

The most common approach to creating business services in a business process layer is to build these services as they are needed. This will inevitably to business services being revisited with requirements that previously, in a different context, were not recognized. Even when your business services have reached maturity, business processes evolve and regulatory requirements sprout, necessitating change to your existing business services.
The changes to business services can be divided into two categories: changes that are limited to the internal workings of a service, and changes that will affect the external interface of a service. For this book, the first category is out of scope. The rest of this chapter is applicable to the external interfaces of business services.

Business service changes can be functional and/or semantic. Functional changes alter the functionality provided by the service, such as:
- Adding or removing functionality to or from a service
- Changing functionality provided by a service

Semantic changes alter the information model used by the service, such as:
- Adding or removing data elements or attributes to or from the information model
- Changing existing data element or attributes in the information model

Service Implementation changes are changes that do not change the service interface, such changes maintain backward compatibility, such as:

- Bug fixes – fixing a faulty functionality of the service
- Performance or scalability improvements – improving nonfunctional aspects of the service
- Technology stack upgrades – changes to the underlying infrastructure upon which the service is implemented

Even when the data interfaces haven't changed, e.g. when the change in a service is only functional, you'll need to be able to identify the new version on the outside, so its service interface will change.

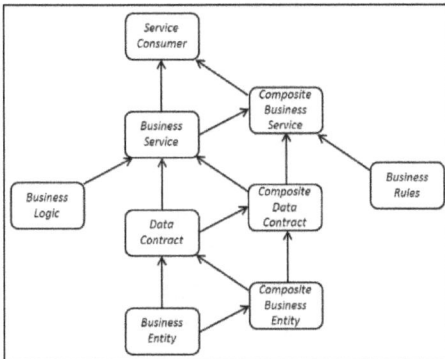

Figure 13: Change propagation in the service stack

All the versionable artifacts of a service will be affected by changes, and these changes will ripple through the artifacts from bottom to top, eventually impacting the service consumers as shown in figure 13. Since the dependencies are not 1:1 but n:m, change propagation to higher levels can easily and quickly reach a very high level of complexity.

While versioning lets you control the effects of changes, compatibility helps you alleviate some of the negative effects of versioning, which is why compatibility is one of the most important aspects when defining changes to interfaces.

The main issue with changes to external interfaces of business services lies in dependencies: if an interface of a service changes, the consumers of the service may need to change too. Whether this consumer change is imperative depends on the compatibility type of the change: we recognize four types:

- No compatibility: known as breaking change
- Backwards compatibility: a new version of a contract that continues to support consumers designed to work with the old version of the contract
- Forwards compatibility: a contract that is designed to support unknown future consumers. In XML terms this is also known as XSD extensibility.
- Back- & Forwards compatibility: the combination of 2 and 3.

Compatibility not just depends on service interface definitions: Improved compatibility can also be provided by the service consumer, which Martin Fowler briefly describes as the *"TolerantReader"* pattern. This pattern describes that the tolerant reader of a message extracts only what it needs from that message and ignores the rest. Rather than implementing a strict validation scheme, it will process messages despite schema violations. Exceptions are thrown only when the message structure prevents the reader from interpreting the message, or the content clearly violates business rules. A tolerant reader will ignore new data elements and attributes and tolerate unexpected data values as long as this information does not provide critical input to the service logic. Implementing this pattern will also ensure a much lower vulnerability to version changes.

It's counterpart, the *"StrictWriter"* pattern is not formally described, but from compatibility point of view just as important: whereas reading messages benefits from fault tolerance, writing messages benefits from strict adherence to message schemas. As a real-world example, if you write a letter, you will want to apply the

"StrictWriter" pattern, meaning grammatically correct and without spelling errors. But if you receive a letter you will want to apply the *"TolerantReader"* pattern, meaning you don't reject the letter as unreadable when it contains a grammar or spelling error. This also illustrates the essential difference between exchanging objects and exchanging messages. If the teleportation device on Starship Enterprise were to exist, it could not afford the slightest mismatch when *digitizing and rematerializing* objects. But when exchanging messages we can and should be much more tolerant.

An often overlooked compatibility aspect is "semantic compatibility", which does not address the structure of the messages, but the meaning of the messages and message elements. The same four compatibility types apply, and it is important to verify whether a change of the meaning of the messages or message elements is involved.

The highly distributed nature, multilayer implementation and increasing integration requirements of most large enterprise systems make a service versioning policy an indispensable requirement. A versioning policy for business services should prescribe which artifacts to version, which version identifiers to assign, when to use which change compatibility type and how to apply version control. A most important aspect of versioning governance is the number of versions that will be supported, which theoretically can vary between one (single version) and indefinite (multiple version). Both approaches have their specific pros and cons:

Single version	
Pros	**Cons**
The service represents one single implementation for a business process, thereby ensuring "re-usability".	Every change may require migration work within the application
Maintenance is greatly simplified	Services and contracts need to be designed with utmost care, to ensure maximum forward and backward compatibility.
The service can have a fixed endpoint URL, so no effort is needed to allow for static or dynamic endpoint URL switching.	Deployment & backout is very sensitive and must be carefully planned with all service consumers.
There is only one version of source code to be maintained.	

Table 11a: Pros and Cons of supporting a single service version only

Multiple versions	
Pros	**Cons**
Changes and enhancements can be made to individual services and released as new versions without causing an impact on the existing service consumers	Multiple versions can quickly lead to a lot of dependency management issues, thereby dramatically increasing complexity
Multiple versioning provides the flexibility to prioritize and migrate to the latest version according to a convenient schedule or budget.	Any bug-fixes at a later point of time would need appropriate fixing in all applicable versions of the service.
Backout planning is easy, just revert to an earlier stable version.	Custom solution would need to be followed in most cases, requiring to maintenance of several versioned copies of the WSDL and schema.

	Some version registry is required to point or redirect to the appropriate endpoint URL
	Source code needs very careful control so that multiple versions of binaries are maintained appropriately.

Table 11b: Pros and Cons of supporting multiple service versions

Both approaches have their specific pros and cons, which makes it very difficult to choose a particular approach. Hence, a best practice recommendation for versioning governance strategy is:

- Use a mix-and-match of both worlds by following versioned services approach, but retain control of the versioning nightmares by limiting the maximum active versions to two.
- When launching a new version of the service, only retain the last of the previous versions. All the lower versions should be deprecated and de-commissioned.
- This means, no more than two active versions of a service will exist at any point of time. Policies need to be established and communicated to the service consumers to ensure that migration is done on time.
- The service owner cannot be held responsible for impacts to a service consumer if the it continues to use a deprecated version of the service.

Another best practice recommendation is to increment major versions for incompatible changes, and increment minor versions for compatible (forwards or backwards) changes.

8 About tooling.

As with all tools, it's not the tool that matters. You can have the best tools in the world, but unless you are a good craftsman who can visualize and create the products you want to make with them, the tools *per se* are useless. Where a poor craftsman blames a tool, the good craftsman succeeds despite a tool. This of course does not deny that the good craftsman can greatly benefit from a good tool.

To adequately support the various message exchange patterns, the set of integration tools should cover quite a list of capabilities, and be able to meet many requirements. Obviously, it should at least cover the entire integration stack.

Integration Stack	Requirements
Authentication & Authorization	Verify the caller's identity and the caller's right to access services, either direct by accessing an identity store (e.g. LDAP) or brokered through a security token (e.g. SAML, OAuth). Forward caller's identity to the service for direct authentication and authorization. Retrieve a security token for caller identity from a security token provider. Forward security tokens to services. Support for API key authentication and authorization. Support for Single Sign-On (SSO)
Transport Protocol	Support for a variety of transport protocols. Principally, every integration service, can and should be made protocol independent, for example through the use of protocol adapters. In practice, the various message exchange patterns have their preferred protocols. An ESB is best implemented with message queueing protocols, an API mgmt. tool will mostly depend on HTTP(S), and MFT's principal protocols will be FTP and SecureFTP.

Transport Security	Transport Security can be supported implicitly through a secure protocol. Over insecure protocols, support is needed to secure transport explicitly through hashing, signing or encryption. For XML/Soap webservices, WS-Security should be supported.
Data Structure	XML, JSON, delimited and positional flat files, business standard formats (e.g. EDI, SWIFT), blobs. Preferably, these data structures can be described by an open schema.
Message Exchange Patterns	All base message exchange patterns must be supported. The SR MEP may benefit from correlation support, where the request is assigned a correlation ID, to allow correlation to a subsequent response. The PS MEP may benefit from a portal where a client can subscribe to certain message types.
Policies	Allows for Policy Management, Policy Enforcement and Policy Monitoring. For XML/Soap webservices, WS-Policy should be supported.
Information type	The typification of the information has no direct consequences for the tooling.
Business Process protocols, Workflow	Provide the means for service composition. The tooling may include support for Business Process protocols such as EDI, SWIFT, HL7 etc. Many integration tools offer process choreography and service orchestration capabilities, even to the point of being able to execute BPEL. See paragraph 8.1 for more information.

Service Level Agreements	Whereas many of the service level requirements can and must be met by correct service design, up to a certain level some of the service level requirements must be met by the tooling. To maximize employability of the tooling, the tooling must be able to meet the highest service level requirements.
Capabilities	**Requirements**
Quality of Service	Whereas some protocols and message exchange patterns are inherently unreliable, the tooling must be able to meet 100% reliability requirements for protocols and message exchange patterns that do support 100% reliability. For XML/Soap webservices, WS-ReliableMessaging should be supported.
Discovery	The tooling must be able to present a service inventory, human readable and machine readable, by which clients can discover what services are available to them. The tooling must also be able to present service meta data, human readable and machine readable, by which clients know how to communicate with the service.
Dynamic configuration	Provide a console to add, change and remove components (endpoints, message types, transformations, routings, etc. . .) dynamically, preferably without disturbing running instances or services. May conflict with an n-tiered deployment process.
Deployment Process	Should provide support for deployment process, both through a UI, such as an installation wizard, and automated through some form of installer.
Deployment flexibility	Various service models may be accommodated, such as on-premise, cloud and SaaS. Hybrid models should also be supported.

SDLC Environments	Should be able to support (or being deployed in) multiple deployment environments; at least a development environment, a testing environment and a production environment must be supported.
Versioning	Should be able to support multiple versions of each service. Should be able to recognize incoming request versions and route to appropriate service version. Should be able to handle versioning errors.
Validation	Must be able to validate messages after receiving and before sending against appropriate schemas.
Transformation	Transform data structures (e.g. json, xml, csv etc...) Transform message structures, mapping from one schema to another.
Dynamic Enrichment	Enrich message content with context data or data dynamically acquired from external sources.
Dynamic Routing	Allow routing to different destinations depending on message context or message content.
Batching / Debatching	Joining several messages to be processed as one whole, or joining several messages into one message. Splitting a message into several parts, to be processed separately, or splitting a message into several messages.
Traffic mediation	Transparent mediation e.g. from SOAP to REST vice versa, from JSON to XML vice versa.
Traffic Shaping / Throttling	Assign different priorities to accelerate or slow down certain channels or message types. Limit data traffic per client, total or per time unit.
Exception handling	Provide a facility to configure and execute exception handling

Alerting	Provide a facility to configure and execute alerting on critical errors, of both the tooling itself and the integration solutions running on the tooling.
Management / Monitoring	Provide a console to manage and monitor the execution of integration services.
Traffic monitoring & Analytics	Natively support traffic monitoring and traffic analysis or connect to 3rd party traffic monitoring systems.
Metering, Billing and Invoicing	Allow metering of data traffic per client, and support billing and invoicing or connect to a billing and invoicing solution.
Track & Trace	Provide a facility to configure message tracking options, to allow identification of individual messages, inspection of their properties and content, and reconstruction of associated events from reception to sending. Provide a facility to replay the execution of a specific instance for debugging purposes.
Operational Integration	System Monitoring, Clustering, Load Balancing, Scalability
Business Process Management	**Requirements**
Business activity monitoring (BAM)	Provide a portal to configure key metrics (KPI's) and monitor business processes over these metrics.
Service composition	Allow creation of less granular services as a composition of more granular services. Provide transaction support over service invocations.
Service Orchestration	See discussion in paragraph 8.1
Process Choreography	
BPEL	

Complex event processing (CEP)	Complex event processing is best addressed by specific tooling, Some integration tools offer limited capability to complex event processing; ideally, they would offer connectivity to a CEP tool.

Table 12: Integration capabilities

8.1 Service Composition, Service Orchestration & Process Choreography

There seems to be no generally accepted definition of the terms "service orchestration" and "process choreography", just as there is little shared understanding of the differences between the two.

For the purpose of this book, the difference is rather academic and of little consequence, so when using either of the terms, both are meant. The one difference that really must be made, is the difference between "service composition" and "service orchestration", where "service composition" creates a new service by combining two or more different services, and "service orchestration" deals with the coordination of two or more different services. This coordination (or orchestration or choreography if you will) implies the use of business logic or business rules. Within this book, "service composition" is the combining of two or more service with no (or a minimum of) business logic. As such, "service composition" is a capability that every integration tool should be able to provide.

When looking at figure 8, there can be little doubt that service orchestration or process choreography must take place in the business process tier. In fact, many commercially available integration tooling will offer (or claim to offer) these capabilities. Some even go so far as to offer the capability to read and execute BPEL (Business Process Execution Language).

The whole purpose of creating a business process tier between user interface and application logic is to maximize business agility by loose coupling. That is why it is of vital importance to apply the principle of loose coupling to all levels of the software stack, from source code to process choreography. As we have seen earlier, the higher the level on which we apply loose coupling, the more effective it is. In other words, nowhere in the software stack is loose coupling more important than in process choreography. This is one reason not to hide your process choreography in your integration tooling, but rather make it explicit in a dedicated workflow tool.

There are two archetypes of process choreography: sequential workflow and state machine.

A sequential workflow represents a predetermined execution of steps. It supports the three basic logic structures in programming "sequence", "selection" and "iteration". This makes variation in execution possible, but not outside predefined paths. Obviously, the name sequential workflow is a bit misleading, but since the generic term workflow by itself is also used to encompass both archetypes, the adjective "sequential" is only used to distinguish it from the generic term.

A (finite) state machine (FSM) represents a set of states, transitions, and actions. The steps in a state machine are triggered by events, and the action that is taken depends on the state of the machine. This mimics real-life processes much better, it is much more flexible and it is the perfect partner to an event driven architecture.

Ironically, integration tools only support sequential workflows, not state machine, which is a much more important reason not to implement process choreography in your integration tooling. To maximize business process agility, rather implement it in a dedicated workflow tool that supports state machines.

A different kind of loose coupling can be achieved be designing business process models in a BPM tool, and exporting the model in

BPEL to be executed by the integration tool. For XML/Soap webservices, WS-BPEL could be supported. Since BPEL only supports sequential workflows, this is not recommended, and even then, a dedicated workflow tool would be a better choice to execute the generated BPEL.

8.2   Integration as a platform

As mentioned earlier, the similarities between data and application integration may warrant to uphold one integration platform to support both types. On the other hand, the differences are fundamental enough to justify for both types to have their own platform: a data integration platform and an application integration platform. Both approaches have their pros and cons. See also table 8.

One platform for AI and DI	
Pros	Cons
Consolidation of tooling: Only one hub to manage and monitor all integration services.	Responsibility conflicts: difficult to separate authorization to AI and DI services.
Easy to connect BI and operational apps to the same integration services.	Operational conflicts: increased chance that execution of DI services may hinder AI services, vice versa.
	Design errors: increased chance of designing inappropriate services

Table 13a: Pros and Cons of one mixed integration platform

Two platforms, one AI, one DI	
Pros	Cons
Each hub has only the tooling it needs.	Crossing the boundary not straightforward: not easy to connect BI and operational apps to the same integration services.

Responsibilities can be clearly defined. Typical DI capabilities (e.g. data cleansing, referential integrity resolution) are unavailable on the AI platform.	Multiple deployments, with the risk of unintentional differences between the hubs.
Reduce design conflicts: separating AI and DI services makes design decisions explicit	More expensive in acquisition and maintenance.
Allows different configuration of shared capabilities.	

Table 13b: Pros and Cons of two separate integration platforms

Probably the best advice is to start with one platform for all integrations, and with increasing maturity, evolve to two separate platforms.

Below is a matrix mapping tooling to message exchange patterns; an important factor is message size. The boundary between small and large messages is always arbitrary, and partly depends on the underlying infrastructure. The maximum message size that the infrastructure for the small messages solutions can accommodate is an absolute boundary that cannot be crossed. The practical boundary is much lower, 100 kilobyte is a commonly adopted boundary. For example, if your messaging infrastructure has a limit of 4 MB per message, and your practical limit is 100 KB, then the following definition applies: small messages are normally less than 100 KB, and never over 4 MB, large message are often larger than 100 KB or can sometimes be over 4 MB.

	MEP	sync	Small Messages	Large Messages
		async	Tooltype	Tooltype
FF	Fire & Forget a.k.a. datagram	async	Message Broker Enterprise Service Bus	Managed File Transfer
RR	Request / Response	sync	API management	

SR	Solicit / Response a.k.a. Request / Callback	async	Message Broker Enterprise Service Bus	Managed File Transfer
PS	Publish / Subscribe a.k.a. Observer	async	Message Broker Enterprise Service Bus	Managed File Transfer

Table 14: Message exchange patterns and Tooling

Tooling types rendered in light-gray are choices that are technically possible, but not recommended. To explain why an Enterprise Service Bus is preferable to a Message Broker, the difference between the two must be clear. Unfortunately, there is no clear definition of either concept. Generally, message brokers are often associated with hub and spoke architecture, while service busses are said to have a bus architecture. Some describe a hub and spoke architecture as *"a centralized broker (hub) and adapters (spokes) which connect applications to the hub. A spoke connects to an application and can convert application data format to a format which the hub understands, and vice versa."* If you were to replace the word "hub" by "bus", and the word "spoke" by "port", you have the description of an ESB architecture. Does this mean the difference is purely textual? *"The hub brokers all messages and takes care of content transformation/translation of the incoming message into a format the destination system understands and routes the message."* is the continuation of the hub and spoke description. Herein lies the main difference: whereas all of the intelligence is concentrated in the hub, and the spokes perform dumb data transport, in the service bus architecture the bus is dumb, and all of the intelligence is concentrated in the ports, which makes the service bus much more flexible and dynamic than the message broker, and therefore the preferred choice as tooling for asynchronous messaging.

As with Message Broker and Enterprise Service Bus, all vendors support their own interpretation of the term API management. Where for one vendor API management is a cloud based portal where clients can host their web services, for the other vendor it is a development environment that lets you design, build and deploy web services. Building, deploying and securing web services without using an API management tool is easy. It is the profusion of non-functional requirements that cause the need for a tool that addresses most or all of these non-functional requirements. Examples of the capabilities that are probably required are Management & Monitoring, Discovery, Version control, Traffic mediation & throttling, Traffic monitoring & Analytics, Metering, Billing and Invoicing, Exception handling and Alerting.

Traditionally, managed file transfer solutions did just what the name suggests: they managed the transfer of files. They managed the point-to-point transfer of files without static or dynamic routing, transformation or enrichment, thereby creating strong interdependencies, with a lot of redundancy in file-based integration solutions, both in design, when designing, building and testing them, as well as in operation, when executing, monitoring and maintaining them. Since the only characteristic that separates the choice for a messaging solution or a file transfer solution is the sizing of the data involved, it is obvious that the principles that govern messaging solutions also unabatedly govern file transfer solutions. This means that a suitable MFT solution should be modeled after a service bus architecture, which disqualifies many to most of today's commercially available MFT solutions.

A common issue with file-based integration is that the MFT solution makes it easy to step outside the boundaries of application integration. Most commercially available MFT solutions will support file transfer to and from humans, which falls outside the scope of application integration. Supporting human endpoints in application integration services will dilute their purpose and may increase complexity manifold: think of the various message exchange patterns that will need to address human endpoints and the consequences for adapters, security, availability etc.

Electronic Data Interchange (EDI).

Electronic Data Interchange (EDI) is the computer-to-computer exchange of business transactions in a standard electronic format that are exchanged between business partners, such as manufacturers and their suppliers.

EDI started off as an expansion on standardized U.S. Army shipping manifests developed in 1948, and the first messages were sent in 1965 by telex. To standardize the formats the Transportation Data Coordinating Committee (TDCC) was formed in 1968 by a group of railroad companies. In 1973 the File Transfer Protocol (FTP) was published, and two years later TDCC released the first EDI standard. In 1978, TDCC becomes the ANSI / X12 committee, who in 1981 released the ANSI / X12 standard. To promote global usage, the UN steps in to release the UN / Edifact standard in 1985. In the meantime other standards branch off, like SWIFT in 1974, and HIPAA in 1996.

Various message types have been defined; the most common are purchase orders, invoices, and advance shipping notices, but many other transactions are available, such as bills of lading, inventory documents, shipping-status documents, and payment documents. These message definitions were not adopted by everyone with the same enthusiasm, which resulted in splitting off various dialects for specific regions or industries, thereby defeating the original goal of standardization. The Unece organization currently recognizes 188 different EDI message types.

Conceptually, four aspects (message format, message transfer protocol, message authentication and business process) bear no relation to each other, but this was unfortunately not explicitly stated in the standards, so we see a lot of implementations where two, three or even all four aspects are tightly coupled, e.g. the Odette EDI standard, which prescribes all four

---

aspects, thus effectively tight-coupling four essentially unrelated elements.

Whereas EDI message structures have evolved only marginally since their inception in the 70ies, the transport protocols have seen dramatic change: the first EDI exchange took place via telex, but soon after EDI messages were exchanged over magnetic tapes. By the end of the 80ies, almost all EDI traffic took place over dial-up or leased phone lines. We had to wait for the turn of the century for the introduction of an internet based protocol. The http(s) based AS2 protocol is now fast becoming the *de facto* standard protocol for EDI messaging.

Many organizations utilize a vendor supplied integration solution to implement their EDI messaging. Inevitably, such a solution provides at least part of the capabilities that can be expected of a full-grown integration hub, but in most cases it is not enough to carry the role of generic integration platform. One choice could be to migrate your existing EDI solution to your generic integration platform; this could require a lot of effort, such as implementing EDI message structures and mappings, specific protocols, business partner management etc. Depending on circumstances, it may be a better option to leave the existing EDI solution in place, but to change its role into either an extension of your generic integration platform, or an adapter to your generic integration platform.

9   The Integration Architect

According to many enterprise architecture frameworks, the enterprise architecture domain is made up of the Business, Data, Application and Technology architecture subdomains, also known as the BDAT model. What is not explicitly mentioned is that these subdomains cannot exist in isolation, they need to be perfectly aligned to be of value. As stated before, it is the integration architect's responsibility to see that enterprise architecture gets implemented in an effective, efficient and equitable manner, not within the various systems and applications (that is the solution architect's responsibility), but across the various systems and applications. Ideally, this means that an experienced enterprise architecture body is in place, and that all of its subdomains are equally and adequately addressed and are aligned. In an organization of this maturity integration is implicitly addressed and the role of the integration architect can be limited to the technological aspects of cross-boundary communications. In fact, as soon as your integration infrastructure is in place and in control, and your integration patterns are in place and proven, the integration architect becomes largely superfluous. Any solution architect should be capable to map enterprise requirements to the existing patterns.

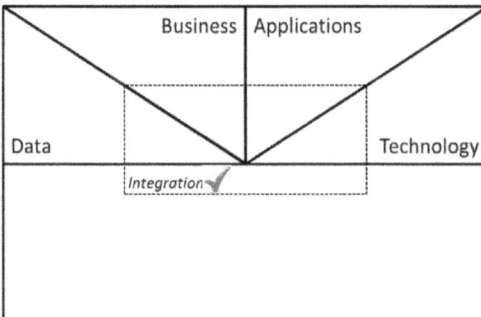

Figure 14: Positioning Integration in the BDAT model

Only when new technologies become available, it is the integration architect's task to establish their potential and possible impact on the existing integration stack, and decide if they should be adopted, where they can fit in, how they should be embedded, and in which scenarios they could or should be utilized.

Often enterprise architecture does not reach this level of maturity. One of its subdomains might not be adequately addressed, there might be insufficient alignment between the subdomains, or the business domain architectures do not fit well together; those are the gaps that the integration architect must fill in.

If enterprise architecture lacks all together, the integration architect faces a choice: either leave the gap as-is and by some means glue the disparate landscape of fragmented solutions together, or try for an integrated landscape of coordinated solutions; this needs filling in the enterprise architecture gap. The first option will make your project managers and solution architects happy, since glueing solutions together will affect the solutions only slightly or not at all. Ultimately, the organization is not helped at all, because this approach threatens the continuity of your primary business processes support. Also, it guarantees that the same problems and issues will keep popping up again and again. More importantly, it harbours the potential of a major break-down, because there is no overview of the interconnections between the solutions.

The second option is where the integration architect establishes a limited enterprise architecture context around integration requests and requirements as they present themselves. He, or she, identifies the business process in which the requirement lives, and may need to model it, then partially defines the data architecture of the information involved, evaluates how involved solutions are affected, selects the technologies to be used, and takes great care that all of this is aligned mutually, aligned with the existing artifacts from previous integration requests, and aligned with the existing system landscape. This, in fact, is a bottom-up approach to enterprise architecture whereby the integration architect, piece by piece, establishes those aspects of an enterprise architecture that are relevant for integration; such an architect is known as a guerilla architect.

9.1 The traditional integration architect

A common description of the integration architect's role is to plan, coordinate, architect, and supervise all activities related to the integration of software programs, applications, and third-party solutions as required to meet the business requirements of the organization. This description is delightfully vague, especially the clause about meeting business requirements, since it is the responsibility of every role within IT to meet business requirements. So where does the responsibility of the integration architect to meet business requirements begin, and where does it end? The issue can be avoided by leaving business requirements to enterprise architects and business analysts, and placing integration architecture in the realm of technology architecture. In this simplistic approach the integration architect is responsible for "middleware", an even more vague term for software that allows other software to interact. For the architect this means evaluating, selecting, implementing, configuring and possibly customizing the "middleware". It also means developing and maintaining an integration architecture blueprint for the organization through the usual architecture artifacts, such as principles, standards, patterns, procedures, guidelines and best practices, and it includes overseeing the interoperability of involved applications, in-house developed as well as commercial off-the-shelf and external third parties, as necessary.

The given definition of "middleware" illustrates the inadequacy of the technology focus, since it implies that if the integration architect succeeds in allowing software to interact, his job is done. At best, allowing software to interact is a prerequisite to integration, meaning that if the integration architect succeeds in allowing software to interact, his job can start.

9.2 The guerilla integration architect

As stated earlier, the guerilla integration architect must be very versatile. On top of the traditional tasks that the integration architect is expected to fulfill, the guerilla architect fills the gap in enterprise architecture. As the requests and requirements for new integrations will arrive with little or no context, this context will have to be established.

So first the guerilla integration architect will need to fill in the missing context in business architecture, by identifying the business process within its settings and produce a baseline model. If the required integration is part of a changing business process, an as-is and a to-be business process model is called for. The required integration must be located within the model; it could form one of the start- or endpoints of the process, fulfill a prerequisite for the process, perform a task within the process, or even represent the entire business process. The actors, events and triggers associated with the integration must be defined, and what business event is triggering the execution of this integration, what does it in turn trigger itself and which actors are involved. The information that is involved in the process must be defined, and business entities must be identified. Finally, quantitative details about frequency, size must be known.

Next, the missing context in data architecture must be filled in. The business entities recognized in the business architecture step must be defined if they weren't described before, or checked for completeness and aptitude if they were. The authoritative sources of the entities, data elements and attributes must be resolved, and a data model must be created, preferably derived from an accepted standard, such as OAG, EDI, SEPA, XBRL, ISO etc. With this information, and the previously established business architecture context, the most suitable message exchange pattern can be selected. Once a message exchange pattern is chosen, corresponding service contracts van be defined, that will be based on the identified business entities' models.

Third, the missing context in application architecture must be filled in. Now that the service contracts are known, the impact on the affected applications must be evaluated. These applications must be able to receive and process the triggers, fire the events, and provide the service endpoints that were identified in the previous steps.

Lastly, the selected message exchange patterns, service contracts and affected applications established in the previous steps must be evaluated against the existing integration reference architecture. If the evaluation reveals a gap in the existing architecture, then that gap must be filled in. It might be that you need to add a new adapter, a new transformation capability, or a new security protocol. This is the traditional area of expertise of the integration architect.

At each step in the process you can find that artefacts, partly or wholly, already are available. When this occurs, you must define whether that artefact can be reused as-is, whether it needs to be changed or amended, or whether it cannot be reused at all. In the second case, you must decide on a change strategy as detailed in chapter 7.3. If an existing artefact cannot be reused at all, then technically you could create a new version, but this is closing your eyes to the underlying causes. You must find out why it cannot be reused, and then decide on the way to go forward.

The whole process is iterative, since you might find that an affected application is not capable of, or not suitable for, a technology that is recommended or required for the selected message exchange pattern. You'll need to backtrack the chain of decisions, possibly all the way back to selecting a different message exchange pattern.

10 Bibliography

Gary Bartlett (2001): *Systemic Thinking*. International Conference on Thinking

R.M. Bastien (2018): *The New Age of Corporate IT*. NAIT Publications

Nicholas Carr (2003): *IT doesn't matter*. Harvard Business Review

Thomas Erl (2005): *Service-Oriented Architecture: Concepts, Technology, and Design*. Prentice Hall

Erich Gamma, John Vlissides, Ralph Johnson, Richard Helm (1994): *Design Patterns*. Addison-Wesley

Jamshid Gharajedaghi (2011): *Systems Thinking: Managing Chaos and Complexity*. Elsevier

Tom Graves (2008): *Bridging the Silos*. Tetradian

Carsten Hentrich & Uwe Zdun (2012): *Process-Driven SOA*. Infosys Press

Francis Heylighen (2009): *Complexity and Self-organization*. Encyclopedia of Library and Information Sciences

Francis Heylighen (2015): *Distributed Intelligence Technologies: present and future applications*. World Scientific

Gregor Hohpe and Bobby Woolf (2003): *Enterprise Integration Patterns*. Addison-Wesley

Jan Hoogervorst (2004): *Enterprise Architecture: Enabling Integration, Agility and Change*. World Scientific Vol.13-03

Jan Hoogervorst (2009): *Enterprise Governance and Enterprise Engineering*. Springer

David S. Linthicum (1999) *Enterprise Application Integration* Addison-Wesley

Edward Lorenz (1963): *Deterministic Nonperiodic Flow*. Journal of Atmospheric Sciences, Vol.20

"The Manifesto Authors" (2009): *SOA Manifesto*. http://www.soa-manifesto.org.

OMG Group (2009): *Service oriented architecture Modeling Language (SoaML).* OMG Group

Andrea Prencipe, Andrew Davies & Mike Hobday (2005): *The Business of Systems Integration.* Oxford University Press

Jeanne Ross, Peter Well & David Robertson (2006): *Enterprise Architecture as a strategy.* Harvard Business Review Press

Marcus Vitruvius (40 - 30 BC): *De Architectura.* Dover Publications

Gerald Weinberg (2001): *An introduction to General Systems Thinking.* Dorset House

Joseph Yoder and Brian Foote (1997) *Big Ball of Mud.* Fourth Conference on Patterns Languages of Programs

www.ingramcontent.com/pod-product-compliance
Lightning Source LLC
Chambersburg PA
CBHW032001190326
41520CB00007B/319